A GAME AT CHESSE

T0382606

𝔄 𝔊𝔞𝔪𝔢 𝔞𝔱 ℭ𝔥𝔢𝔰𝔰𝔢

BY

THOMAS MIDDLETON

EDITED

BY

R. C. BALD

CAMBRIDGE

AT THE UNIVERSITY PRESS

MCMXXIX

CAMBRIDGE
UNIVERSITY PRESS

University Printing House, Cambridge CB2 8BS, United Kingdom

Cambridge University Press is part of the University of Cambridge.

It furthers the University's mission by disseminating knowledge in the pursuit of education, learning and research at the highest international levels of excellence.

www.cambridge.org
Information on this title: www.cambridge.org/9781107487437

© Cambridge University Press 1929

This publication is in copyright. Subject to statutory exception and to the provisions of relevant collective licensing agreements, no reproduction of any part may take place without the written permission of Cambridge University Press.

First published 1929
First paperback edition 2015

A catalogue record for this publication is available from the British Library

ISBN 978-1-107-48743-7 Paperback

Cambridge University Press has no responsibility for the persistence or accuracy of URLs for external or third-party internet websites referred to in this publication, and does not guarantee that any content on such websites is, or will remain, accurate or appropriate.

To

SIR ARCHIBALD STRONG

CONTENTS

PREFACE

IT is no exaggeration to say that more is known about *A Game at Chesse* than about any other pre-Restoration play. In spite of the uncertainty that must attend any attempt to interpret all the details of the allegory, the general trend of its political satire is clear. It is the last expression of that great outburst of national feeling to which the Elizabethan age owed so much of its inspiration, although it is true that the spirit of independence and high adventure has narrowed down into a political and religious hatred of Spain. The poetry and rhetoric of Shakespeare's historical plays have given place to satire, for, as Swinburne says, this play is "the only work of English poetry which may properly be called Aristophanic."

However, it is in connection with the stage history of the play that our knowledge is most detailed; even the dates of its allowance by the Master of the Revels, and of the first and last performances, are all known. Its suppression by the authorities, and the consequent surreptitious circulation of copies, both manuscript and printed, have had the result that an editor is confronted with a series of texts unique in their interest. It is a matter of some importance that those who have been engaged on the study of Shakespearian texts are beginning to find that the method of inferring the nature of the original manuscripts from the printed quarto or folio has its limitations, and that valuable aid can be obtained from the study of the extant manuscripts of plays of the other writers of the period. The four manuscripts of *A Game at Chesse*, which provide transcripts in the hands of the author and two scribes working under his direction, offer exceptional material for the study of certain types of dramatic texts.

The two previous modern editions of the play are those contained in the collected works of Middleton by Dyce

ix

Preface

(1840) and Bullen (1886). Dyce did good service by showing which was the more reliable of the quartos, and indicated that the inferior quartos could often correct it when it was wrong; he also collated the Lansdowne and Bridgewater MSS., and did the pioneer work in identifying the characters of the play. Bullen half-heartedly collated the Trinity MS., indicated incompletely some of Middleton's sources, and attempted the identification of as many more of the characters as he could, but Dyce's editing was, none the less, the basis of his work. Perhaps if he had been successful in his search for MS. Malone 25 he would have realised the importance of the Trinity MS. and based his text on it. The important developments in the textual study of the early drama which have occurred in the last few years, as well as the extensive illustrations from contemporary pamphlets added here, will, it is hoped, justify the present edition.

I desire to acknowledge gratefully the freely-given advice and assistance of Dr W. W. Greg, who also lent me his copy of one of the quartos of the play; of Mr F. P. Wilson and Mr Percy Simpson of Oxford; and of Mr A. L. Attwater of Pembroke College, Cambridge. Clare College generously gave me a grant to defray the cost of certain necessary photostatic reproductions; the officials of the Trinity College Library have aided me in every way in their power; the Society of the Inner Temple has kindly given me permission to include two previously unpublished extracts from a MS. in its Library; and the Henry E. Huntington Library has allowed me to make full use of the MS. of the play in its possession.

R. C. B.

Cambridge
14 December 1926

ADDENDUM

Just as the final corrections are being made to the proofs of this book there comes the news that another manuscript of *A Game at Chesse* has been found, and was sold at auction at Sotheby's on April 4, 1928. Dr Greg informs me that it is in the hands of two scribes, neither of them either of the scribes concerned in the other manuscripts, but that, like the Bridgewater-Huntington MS., it has an autograph title-page.

R. C. B.

The University of Adelaide
South Australia
8 June 1928

ILLUSTRATIONS

INTRODUCTION

HISTORICAL BACKGROUND

I

A MAN who was born in the same year as Shakespeare and was alive at the accession of Charles I must have lived to see many changes. His adult life would have covered the whole of the period of that great outburst of literary and dramatic activity which is generally grouped together under the designation "Elizabethan," although it extended, roughly, from the publication of *The Shepheardes Calender* in 1579 to the death of James I. But the average man was, then as now, doubtless more deeply stirred by events that were political and national rather than literary, and the patriotism which found its expression in Shakespeare's historical plays, no less than in *The Faerie Queene* or Raleigh's account of the last fight of the *Revenge*, reached its apexes in three great outbursts of national rejoicing. These were the defeat of the Spanish Armada, the discovery of the Gunpowder Plot, and the return of Prince Charles from Madrid in 1624 without a Spanish bride. The third event aroused the last manifestation of the intense spirit that had animated Elizabethan England; thenceforward the eyes of the nation were turned inwards upon itself, and with the growth of the power of Parliament domestic affairs consumed all those energies that had previously found a wider expression.

The fears which the defeat of the Armada in 1588 dispelled for Protestantism in England returned with greater strength in the reign of James I. The counter-Reformation had won great successes abroad, and the outbreak of the Thirty Years' War seemed to many to threaten the complete overthrow of the Protestant cause. The King's

B C

ambitions to hold the balance between the two creeds, and to reconcile them sufficiently so that Catholic and Protestant nations could live together in peace, filled the average Englishman with dismay, for to him the thing was as impossible as a truce between God and the devil. The Gunpowder Plot had arisen from the disappointment of the Catholic hopes in the new sovereign, and, although subsequent events showed that James was willing to make considerable concessions, the memory of the Plot rankled in the minds of his subjects, and would have kept alive the popular hatred against the Catholics, even if the growth of their power abroad had not raised new fears.

There was a nobility of purpose behind James' diplomatic efforts that few of his contemporaries were capable of understanding, but his weakness and his many vacillations made his efforts unavailing, so that eventually his ineffectual embassies became the scorn of Europe. It is difficult, too, to distinguish the noble motives from the sordid ones, for James' desire to secure peace through a marriage alliance of the greatest Catholic with the greatest Protestant reigning house cannot be altogether separated from his desire to obtain a large dowry, with which he hoped to be able to pay off some of his debts. It is no wonder, then, that the King was misunderstood by his subjects, whose instincts were still guided by a fear of Spanish domination. They looked askance at, and finally execrated, the influence of Gondomar, and their mistrust deepened still further at the favours shown to the Catholics. In 1622 orders were issued to restrain preachers from expressing their feelings too openly from the pulpit, and at the same time large numbers of Catholic prisoners were released:

> the Jayles flew open (without miracle)
> And let the locusts out, those dangerous Flies
> Whose propertie is to burne Corne with touching;
> The Heretique Granaries feele it to this minute,
> And now they haue got amongst the Countrie-Crops

Historical Background

They stick so fast to the conuerted Eares
The lowdest Tempest that Authoritie Rowzes
Will hardlie shake 'em off.[1]

Pamphlets denouncing Catholic and Spaniard poured from the presses; advice was proffered and strictures were passed on the King's policy from every side; and suppression only drove men like Thomas Scott[2] across the water to Holland, where they continued their pamphleteering with unabated vigour.

When it was learnt that Charles and Buckingham had secretly departed on February 18, 1623 on their adventurous journey to Madrid, the popular fears increased tenfold, for the danger appeared much closer and therefore more real. Apprehension was not allayed by Charles' long absence, particularly as it was known that efforts were being made to persuade him to change his religion.

All the world wishes him here again [wrote Chamberlain] for the Spanish delayes are like to weare out his patience... besides, there is *periculum in mora* in many wayes, specially in regard of his religion, wch is no small daunger considering his age, the cunning of those he hath to deale wth all, and other circumstance.[3]

It was not till more than three months after this letter was written that Charles set foot on English soil again, and public anxiety had in the meanwhile been raised to a fever heat. The sense of national relief was enormous; the people did not ask if there were any engagements to which the Prince of Wales had pledged himself—they realised only the fact that he had returned in safety and without a bride. At no other period of his life was Charles so popular, and the welcome he received in London was all the more remarkable for being so spontaneous. Wealthy citizens gave banquets in the streets outside their houses to all who

---

[1] Act III, sc. i, ll. 92–99.   [2] The author of *Vox Populi*.
[3] Chamberlain to Carleton, June 28, 1623 (*S.P. (Dom.), James I*, vol. 147, no. 80).

passed by, and bonfires were lit on every available open space. Taylor the Water-Poet wrote enthusiastically:

> The Bels proclaim'd aloud in euery Steeple,
> The ioyfull acclamations of the people.
> The Ordnance thundred with so high a straine,
> As if great *Mars* they meant to entertaine.
> The Bonfires blazing, infinite almost,
> Gaue such a heat as if the world did roast.
> True mirth and gladnesse was in euery face,
> And healths ran brauely round in euery place;
> That sure I thinke this sixt day of October,
> Ten thousand men will goe to bed scarce (&c.)
> This was a day all dedicate to Mirth,
> As 'twere our Royall CHARLES his second birth:
> And this day is a Iewell well return'd
> For whom this Kingdome yesterday so mourn'd.
> God length his dayes who is the cause of this,
> And make vs thankfull for so great a blisse.[1]

So triumphant an occasion was not soon forgotten, and several years later an item on the books of Pembroke Hall, Cambridge, bears witness that the anniversary of the Prince's return was still being celebrated:

Pro igne gratulatorio in anniversarii memoria reditus Principis Caroli ex Hispania ....2*s.* 6*d.*[2]

II

This is not the place to recount the long and tortuous course of the negotiations for the Spanish match, nor to show how they were affected by the events of the Thirty Years' War and reacted, in their turn, on the fortunes of the English Catholics. *A Game at Chesse* has little to do with the *minutiae* of historical truth, so carefully recorded in Gardiner's well-known work, for by the very nature of things, anyone in Middleton's position could not have had access to the true facts. The play is primarily the expression of current popular feelings; it is the embodiment of the prejudices of the multitude, who were incapable of grasping

[1] J. Taylor, *Works* (fo. 1630), p. 102.
[2] Treasurer's Accounts, 1626–7.

4

more than one idea at a time, and whose line of thought was based not so much on principle as on instinct. Yet there is something to be said for the blind hatred which regarded Gondomar as the incarnation of evil, and the narrow mentality which, in its inability to comprehend the motives of de Dominis, could find him nothing but an "arch-hypocrite." Popular prejudice had in these cases gone down to essentials, and it was well for England that the aims of both men were thwarted.

As early as 1611 James had asked for the hand of a Spanish princess for his eldest son, Henry, but the negotiations came to nothing. In 1613, however, a new Spanish ambassador, Don Diego Sarmiento da Acuña (later Count Gondomar), arrived in England, and in 1614 the project of a marriage alliance with Spain was revived through the influence of the King's reigning favourite, Somerset. As early as December 1614 it had been suggested by Sarmiento that Prince Charles (Henry had died in 1612) should visit Madrid, and by the middle of 1615 James had practically agreed to the Spanish terms. The negotiations were interrupted by the fall and disgrace of Somerset, but in 1616 they were again renewed. Raleigh's ill-fated expedition to Guiana interrupted them once more, but Gondomar's firmness prevented the breaking off of diplomatic relations between the two countries, and ultimately led Raleigh to the block. Gondomar returned to Spain in triumph, but meanwhile the Thirty Years' War broke out and James, who was attempting to act as mediator, became more convinced than ever that a close alliance between England and Spain was the only road to the peace of Europe, and the Spaniards themselves were only too glad to continue negotiations for a marriage treaty in order to prevent a breach with England. The war party in England was strong, and the only way they could be overridden was by holding out hopes of the marriage to the King. In 1620 Gondomar returned to England, and he was not long in regaining his influence over James. When he left England two years later he had also a firm adherent in Buckingham, so that, however much the people of England might desire it, an immediate rupture with Spain was impossible. But the triumph of his diplomacy came nearly a year later when Charles and Buckingham accepted his repeated invitation, and set out together for Madrid.

No foreign ambassador, before or since, has ever exerted so much influence in England as Gondomar did. He was directly responsible for the execution of Sir Walter Raleigh, the last of the great Elizabethan sea-captains; he was the means of obtaining large concessions for the Catholics, who for a while enjoyed greater freedom than they had known for many years; but, above all, he succeeded in keeping England at peace with Spain, although the majority of the people had been eager for war since 1617. His tact, his wit, and his keen perception of character enabled him to influence James and Buckingham alike; his charm of manner no less than his power made him eagerly sought after in Court circles, but beyond the Court his influence was regarded with the deepest suspicion. Yet he seems to have been capable of kindness and generosity and to have acquired a real fondness for England. Howell records that while Charles was in Spain:

Count *Gondamar* helpt to free some *English* that were in the Inquisition in *Toledo* and *Sevill*, and I could alledge many instances how ready and chearfull he is to assist any *Englishman* whatsoever, notwithstanding the base affronts he hath often receivd of the *London buys* as he calls them.[1]

But the public ear was deaf to such accounts as this. Gondomar's vivacity seemed but the mask which concealed schemes for the overthrow of everything that England valued; he was the personification of the unholy ambitions of Spain and the abominable perversions of the Papacy. "The cunning Don," says Fuller, "so carried himself in the twilight of *jest-earnest* that with his *jests* he pleased His MAJESTY of England, and with his *earnest* he

[1] *Familiar Letters* (1645), sec. 3, p. 80.

pleasured his Master of *Spain*."[1] The figure of Gondomar, as the Black Knight, is drawn with great gusto and satiric force in *A Game at Chesse*; he dominates the play, and his chuckling speeches of sardonic self-revelation must undoubtedly have been its principal attraction. Here is the full-length portrait of the Gondomar of popular imagination, the man whom "starlings and parrots were first taught to curse."

III

Although Protestantism seemed to many to be losing ground all over Europe during James' reign, it gained for a time one notable convert. This was Marco Antonio de Dominis, Archbishop of Spalatro.[2] Educated by the Jesuits at Padua, he had found the repressive discipline of the order too strict for his active mind, and he turned aside to seek ecclesiastical preferment elsewhere. He became Bishop of Segnia, and eventually Archbishop of Spalatro and primate of his native province, Dalmatia, which was part of the territory belonging to Venice. According to Goodman, de Dominis "was a man of a very deep understanding and of an unquiet spirit."[3] He became an intimate of the great Paolo Sarpi, author of the *History of the Council of Trent*,[4] and with Sarpi vigorously upheld the cause of Venice in its quarrel with Pope Paul V in 1606. It was while he was engaged in refuting some of the pamphlets that were written against Venice at that time that he re-read the works of the early Fathers, in order to examine more closely the basis of the papal authority, and these studies convinced him that the popes had systematically usurped authority that did not belong to them. This, he realised, had been the principal cause of the schisms o. the Reformation, and he bent his energies to evolve a

---

[1] *Church History of Britain* (1655), bk x, p. 100.

[2] The name of his see appears as *Spalato* or *Spoletta* in all the English writings of the period.

[3] *Court and Times of James I*, vol. i, p. 341.

[4] De Dominis brought the manuscript of this famous book to England, where it was published in 1617.

scheme whereby the unity of the Church might be re-established; in outward form, at any rate, it should be one, although there might be considerable differences of thought within it. He developed his ideas with a great wealth of learning in the three large volumes of his book *De Republica Ecclesiastica*, which, however, he did not yet dare to publish, even under the protection of Venice. Meanwhile, through Sarpi he had become acquainted with Bedell, the saintly chaplain of Sir Henry Wotton who was then the English ambassador at Venice, and from Bedell he had heard in full the doctrines of the Church of England. In 1616 he determined to leave Italy and go to a country where it would be possible to spread his ideas more widely. He travelled rapidly to Holland, until he was out of the reach of papal emissaries, and, on reaching the Hague, went to Sir Dudley Carleton, the English ambassador, who assured him that James would welcome him warmly if he crossed over into his dominions.

Encouraged by these assurances, de Dominis landed in England not long afterwards. He was received with every honour; he was given apartments in Lambeth Palace, and in a short time was appointed Dean of Windsor and Master of the Savoy. He published his *magnum opus*, and busied himself with a number of pamphlets against Rome. But soon the nine days wonder of his conversion died down, and it was not long before Englishmen began to realise that his ways were not theirs. He discovered flaws in the leases of some of his tenants at the Savoy, and proposed to eject them; he even presented himself to a living in the gift of the Dean of Windsor. He was eager for further advancement, and when a report of the death of Toby Matthew, the Archbishop of York, reached his ears,[1] he

---

[1] The old Archbishop used to spread these reports himself in order to enjoy hearing of the suitors who had petitioned to be his successor. Fuller, in recording his death, remarks: "He dyed *yeerly* in report, and I doubt not, that in the Apostles sense he *dyed dayly* in his mortifying meditations. He went over the graves of many who looked for his Archbishoprick; I will not say they catched a cold waiting barefoot for a living mans shoes" (*Church History*, bk xi, p. 133).

hastened to Theobalds to ask the King for the vacant see. James very properly replied that he would never think of appointing a foreigner to such a dignity; but the incident shows only too clearly the opinion de Dominis had of his own merits. It must have disappointed him deeply, too, to find that his ideas for the reunion of the Church were no nearer fulfilment; Englishmen understood and applauded him when he denounced the faults of Rome, but his proposals for reunion were incomprehensible to most of them, and nothing more than a vague dream to the more advanced Arminians among them.

Meanwhile changes had occurred in Italy. Paul V was dead, and he had been succeeded by Gregory XV, who had been a friend of de Dominis in his younger days. De Dominis felt that he might find conditions there more favourable to him than they had been before; perhaps, too, as he suggests in a letter to James,[1] he was genuinely homesick—he missed his old friends, and was oppressed by the dull English climate. He therefore determined (in 1622) to return, and doubtless before he announced his intentions he corresponded secretly with the Pope and the various Catholic powers from whom he required safe-conducts. When he asked James to be allowed to depart, the King was exceedingly angry, and it was with considerable difficulty that he eventually obtained the required permission. He tried to convey away the goods he had amassed in this country among the baggage of a departing ambassador,[2] but they were seized at Dover, and only restored to him after the most piteous pleading. On the other side of the Channel de Dominis was warmly welcomed, and the Pope placed a retinue at his disposal for his journey through Italy. But his good fortune did not last for long, for his old friend died a few months afterwards and a new Pope was elected. De Dominis spent the last year of his life in confinement; after his death he was

[1] The letter is printed in Fuller's *Church History*, bk x, p. 96.
[2] There is a reference to this incident in the play at III, i, 337–340.

found guilty of heresy, and his body was disinterred and burnt.

The character of such a man easily lends itself to satire, and in its details the figure of the Fat Bishop is nearer to its original than that of the Black Knight. There is no doubt that de Dominis was a prey to vaulting ambition, and he had given several startling examples of his covetousness. Admitting, as we must, that he possessed these qualities, it was only natural that his return to Rome should lay him open to the charge of hypocrisy. The truth, however, is that de Dominis fell between two stools; or to change the metaphor, he could cut his cloth neither to the Roman nor to the Protestant pattern, though he tried to fit both. Perhaps the aptest remark made concerning him was that of Bishop Andrewes soon after he came to England; someone had asked Andrewes if de Dominis were a Protestant: "Truly I know not," he replied, "but I think he is a detestant of most of the opinions of Rome."[1]

IV

Gondomar and de Dominis are the two outstanding figures in the main plot of Middleton's play. Of the other characters who can be identified much less need be said. The White King is clearly James; there is a considerable strain of flattery infused into the speeches put into his mouth, but to the modern reader they are long-winded, sententious, and dull—for virtue is always less interesting than vice. The White Knight is Charles, and the White Duke is Buckingham;[2] these two are little more than spectators in the earlier part of the play, but the visit to Madrid is allegorically portrayed in iv,iv, v,i and v,iii, and the White Knight gains the final victory by giving check-mate by discovery—a reference to the hostility towards Spain which Charles and Buckingham showed after their return.

[1] Bacon's *Apophthegms*, no. 158.
[2] Bullen is wrong in identifying the White Duke with Charles and the White Knight with Buckingham, as Ward (*Eng. Dram. Lit.* vol. II, pp. 530–1) and Morris (*Eng. Stud.* Band xxxviii (1907), pp. 43–45) have shown.

Historical Background

On the other side, the Black King is Philip IV of Spain and the Black Duke Olivares, his chief minister. The White Bishop is Archbishop Abbot, and the Black Bishop is expressly stated to be the Father General of the Jesuits. The two Queens have generally been taken to represent the consorts of the two Kings, but I am inclined to follow Fleay[1] in identifying them with the Churches of England and Rome. Queen Anne had been dead five years when the play was written, and, although Middleton shows little regard in the play for historical sequence, it is not likely that he would have introduced one dead so long, nor is it easy to believe that he would have referred so openly to her dealings with Catholicism when his attitude to the other members of the Royal Family is so full of respect. If the White Queen is Anne of Denmark, it is difficult to explain why the Black King so vehemently "longs for her prostitution," and should employ the Fat Bishop to attack her. Surely the attack of the Fat Bishop is a reference to the pamphlet that de Dominis wrote against the Church of England after his return, while her rescue by the White Bishop refers to the letter which Abbot was supposed to have written to the King while Charles was in Spain, protesting against the toleration which was to be shown to the Catholics under the terms of the proposed marriage treaty.[2]

The White King's Pawn I take to be Lionel Cranfield, Earl of Middlesex, who began life as a city apprentice and rose to be Lord Treasurer of the realm. His humble origin and his elevation to high rank are clearly referred to in the White King's speech at III, i, 301–9:

> Has my Goodnes
> Clemencie, loue, and fauour gratious raysed thee
> From a Condition next to popular labour,
> Tooke thee from all the dubitable hazards
> Of Fortune, her most vnsecure aduentures

[1] *Biog. Chron.* vol. II, p. 106.
[2] The letter was a forgery: it is printed in Gardiner's *History*, vol. V, pp. 71–72.

And grafted thee into a Branch of honor[1]
And dost thou fall from the Top-bough by the rottennes,
Of thy alone Corruption, like a Fruite
That's ouer ripend by the beames of Fauour?

When Charles and Buckingham returned from Madrid, full of hostility against Spain, Middlesex was the only member of the Council who was firm in his opposition to their desire for war.[2] He well knew what havoc a war would make in the Treasury, and he aroused Charles' enmity by suggesting that even if he did not like the Infanta he should fulfil his obligations honourably, for the credit of the nation. It was widely believed that to save himself from ruin Middlesex had supplied information against Buckingham to Inijosa, the Spanish ambassador, who was intriguing for the favourite's downfall in a last attempt to avert war. Buckingham was accused of conspiring with the Parliament to dethrone James for his opposition to a war with Spain, but by the irony of fate Middlesex's name became connected with the plot in popular rumour.[3] Middlesex's consequent unpopularity on all sides soon led to his downfall; he was impeached, found guilty, and deprived of his offices, although he was only charged with peculation, as Buckingham was afraid of a too thorough sifting of the Spanish question[4].

V

The underplot, of which the White Queen's, Black Queen's and Black Bishop's Pawns are the principal figures, does not admit of the same interpretation as a

---

[1] Does this refer merely to Middlesex's earldom, or to his marriage with Anne Brett, a cousin of Buckingham's mother?

[2] His opposition to a Spanish war is referred to at i, i, 348–352.

[3] See Gardiner, *History*, vol. v, p. 228, and the letter from D. Carleton to Carleton in *S.P. (Dom.), James I*, vol. 164, no. 12.

[4] Previously the White King's Pawn had been identified (by Bullen and others) with Sir Toby Matthew, the son of the Archbishop of York, who had been a friend of Gondomar and became a Jesuit. Professor E. C. Morris, however, maintains that the White King's Pawn is the Earl of Bristol.

piece of historical allegory as the main plot does.[1] This part of the play is merely an *exposé* in general terms of the methods of the Jesuits; the characters are types rather than individuals, and one is hardly justified in accepting Bullen's identification of the Black Bishop's Pawn with the priest John Floyd. Floyd's name meant little to the majority of the audience; the generic name *Jesuit* conveyed far more, and the Black Bishop's Pawn is simply intended to be a representative of the order, bent on corrupting the members of the Church of England, who are typified in the White Queen's Pawn.

The sources for a number of the incidents of this part of the play are to be found in some of the contemporary pamphlets against the Catholics. The Black Bishop's Pawn's attempt to "render pliant" the White Queen's Pawn by means of the tract on obedience is taken straight from Thomas Robinson's pamphlet called *The Anatomie of the English Nunnerie at Lisbon* (1622).[2] The second attempt on the White Queen's Pawn, by means of the vision in the magic glass, makes use of a stage device that had been employed previously in Rowley's play *A Shoo-maker a Gentleman*; the incident was probably suggested to Middleton by the number of conversions to Catholicism by means of faked miracles and visions which were exposed in many of the pamphlets, notably John Gee's *Foote out of the Snare* and *New Shreds of the Old Snare* (1624), and the appearance of the Black Bishop's Pawn in the guise of a gallant is founded directly on a passage in Gee. The gelding of the

---

[1] Professor E. C. Morris, in his paper "The Allegory of *A Game at Chesse*" (*Eng. Stud.* Band XXXVIII (1907), pp. 39–52) tries to show that this part of the play contains references to the Thirty Years' War. The gelding of the White Bishop's Pawn, for instance, refers to Frederick's loss of the Palatinate; and he also suggests that the White Queen's Pawn is the Princess Elizabeth, the Black Queen's Pawn the Archduchess Isabella, the Black Knight's Pawn the Emperor Ferdinand, and the Black Bishop's Pawn Maximilian of Bavaria. But this interpretation, as Morris himself admits, breaks down at several points. There is, however, what seems to be a veiled allusion to the loss of the Palatinate at II, ii, 128–130.

[2] The relevant passages from the pamphlets to which Middleton was indebted are quoted in full in the notes.

Introduction

White Bishop's Pawn may have arisen from Middleton's determination to use the *Taxa Penitentiaria*; he set himself to think of some particularly heinous sin that is not mentioned there, so as to give piquancy to the Black Knight's Pawn's attempts to seek absolution, and so had to introduce the sin into the earlier part of the plot. Finally, the *dénouement*, in which the Black Queen's Pawn thwarts the Black Bishop's Pawn's aims, is an ingenious application of the Ignatian morals expounded in ll. 67–84 of the Induction.

VI

Middleton's debt to contemporary pamphlets, it will be seen, is much more considerable than has previously been realised. Not only do the passages given in Bullen's notes indicate a mere fraction of Middleton's indebtedness to the sources quoted from there, but the list of pamphlets must also be added to, and is probably still incomplete. The more important sources of the play are Thomas Scott's two tracts *Vox Populi* (1620) and *The Second Part of Vox Populi* (1624) and Thomas Robinson's *The Anatomie of the English Nunnerie at Lisbon* (1622)—all of which are mentioned by Bullen—while for information on special topics Middleton drew largely on *A Declaration of the Variance betweene the Pope and the Segniory of Venice* (1606) and *Newes from Rome: Spalato's Doome* (1624). From a number of other pamphlets his borrowing was not so extensive, but he was indebted for an occasional fact, phrase, or idea to *The Friers Chronicle* (entered *S.R.* September 20, 1622), *The State Mysteries of the Jesuites* (dated 1623, but entered *S.R.* October 14, 1622), and to John Gee's *Foote out of the Snare* (entered *S.R.* May 1, 1624). Middleton had also seen (unless he had found similar information elsewhere) *The Downfall of the Jesuits* (1612), and *An Experimentall Discoverie of Spanish Practises* (1623), and may just possibly have had time to see Gee's *New Shreds of an Old Snare* (entered *S.R.* May 24, 1624) and Reynolds' *Vox Coeli* (1624).[1]

[1] See Appendix A, no. 1.

14

Historical Background

This list is a long one, but it shows clearly how intense was Middleton's interest in the burning question of the day. It proves, too, with what haste *A Game at Chesse* was completed. The play was licensed by Sir Henry Herbert on June 12; Gee's *Foote out of the Snare* was only entered on the Stationers' Register on May 1, while *The Second Part of Vox Populi*, to which Middleton was probably more indebted than to any other book, actually contains a reference to Gee's pamphlet.[1] The fashion in which he copies it almost *verbatim* may well be taken as a sign that he had not had time to digest its material properly, and the fact that Gondomar's speech at iv, ii, 43–77 (where Scott is followed most closely) is little more than a repetition at greater length of the soliloquy in iii, i, may perhaps indicate that Middleton was already at work on the play when he read Scott's book.

It is natural that in a play dealing with contemporary political events this constant indebtedness to pamphlets should be found, for many of them, especially those such as *A Declaration of the Variance betweene the Pope and the Segniory of Venice* and *Newes from Rome: Spalato's Doome*, fulfilled the functions of the modern newspaper, and for the ordinary man were his only means of obtaining information, other than by hearsay, of what was happening abroad. In general, it is interesting to compare Middleton's use of his sources with that of the authors of *Sir John van Olden Barnavelt*. This, too, is a play dealing with contemporary history, and Miss Frijlinck, in the section on the sources in her edition of the play, shows that Fletcher and Massinger have derived practically all their information from the news contained in the current pamphlets. She analyses the relation of the play to some eight or nine of them, and points out that Massinger tends far more than Fletcher to turn the actual words of the pamphlet into blank verse.

Finally, the indebtedness of *A Game at Chesse* to two

---

[1] On p. 32.

earlier plays must not be ignored. Its connection with Rowley's *A Shoo-maker a Gentleman* has already been noticed, but it is also of considerable interest to observe that the "dissimulation" of the White Knight in the last scene is certainly modelled on the test imposed by Malcolm on Macduff in iv, iii of *Macbeth*. So, whatever Middleton's connection may have been with the mysterious additions to the witch scenes, there can be no doubt that he was thoroughly familiar with the play.

VII

A Game at Chesse is one of the latest plays of Middleton. Soon after 1620, when he was appointed City Chronologer, Middleton's dramatic activities grew appreciably less. It is true that this is the period of his two great plays, *Women Beware Women* and *The Changeling*, but there seems to be little doubt that he fulfilled his civic duties with a conscientiousness that made the laxity of his successor, Ben Jonson, all the more noticeable. The composing and organising of mayoral pageants, shows, and entertainments laid large claims on his time, and the antiquary Oldys, in a marginal note in his copy of Langbaine's *Dramatic Poets*,[1] mentions that early in the eighteenth century two manuscripts of Middleton's were put up for sale, which contained: "*Annales*: or a Continuation of Chronologie; conteyninge Passages and Occurrences proper to the Hono^ble Citty of London: Beginninge in the Yeare of our Lorde 1620" and "*Middleton's Farrago*"—a collection of notes on political events. His office as City Chronologer may have stimulated Middleton's interest in public affairs; in any case, *A Game at Chesse* is the natural outcome of his activities during the last period of his life.

One of the chief qualities of Middleton's early comedies was his skill in inventing striking and effective situations, and we can see the same skill in the cleverness with which the allegory is sustained in *A Game at Chesse*. In the main,

---

[1] In the British Museum.

the plot is slender; the story of the attempts of the Black Bishop's Pawn to seduce the White Queen's Pawn extends for the whole length of the play, but, for the rest, the plot is made up of a number of isolated incidents, such as the Black Knight's plot against the Fat Bishop, and the journey of the White Knight to visit the Black House. It is clear that for the spectators the centre of interest lay in the biting satire with which the characters of the Black Knight and the Fat Bishop are portrayed.

Satire in drama is the most effective of all means of satire; you cannot show up a man more effectively than by making him appear to do it himself. It is the seeming self-revelation, with the apparent absence of comment, that gives so much relish to the figures of Gondomar and de Dominis in the play; when the Black Knight boasts of his plots that

> All these, and ten times trebled, has this braine
> Beene parent to,

or when the Fat Bishop meditates that

> I am perswaded that this Flesh would fill
> The biggest Chayre Ecclesiasticall
> If it were put to Tryall,

they carry conviction home to the mind in a way that no amount of denunciation could have done. None of the other characters is half so lifelike. The Black Bishop's Pawn is drawn to a far meaner scale—he is merely the villain of a melodrama; the Black Queen's Pawn has some breath of life in her, and the White Queen's Pawn is virtuous without being utterly dull. The rest, even the White Knight and the White Duke, are simply puppets, or rather, they are merely the chess-men which the author moves across the board as the progress of the game impels him.

Middleton was not a lyric poet in the way that most of the Elizabethan dramatists were; in spirit he is more akin to the eighteenth century than they, and his satiric methods anticipate those of Dryden. Yet occasionally there leaps out a passage that none but a true poet could have written:

> that Eye
> Do's promise single life and meeke obedience;
> Uppon those lips, the sweete fresh Buds of youth,
> The holie Dewe of prayer lyes like pearle
> Dropt from the opening Eye-lids of the Morne
> Uppon the bashfull Rose;

and the following few lines, like those earlier ones spoken by the Black Queen's Pawn:

> hee will cherish
> All his yong Tractable sweete obedient daughters
> E'en in his bosome, in his owne deare bosome

have a sinister suggestiveness that is fully justified by the subsequent course of events. At times, too, a deeper meditative note is heard:

> Wee do not alwayes feele our fayth wee liue by,
> Nor euer see our Growth, yet both worke upward.

Middleton possessed a considerable command of imagery, and he often uses a biting metaphor, simile, or phrase to give point to his satire, although to remove them from their context is generally to lose half their force. His style is fluent, and his verse is of the easy conversational type of which Fletcher was a master, but he was never exuberant. He never played fast and loose with the double meaning of a word as his frequent collaborator, Rowley, could never resist doing; and III, ii is a good example of Middleton's cruder horse-play. The power of condensation was also Middleton's, as one can see at a glance by comparing the Black Knight's long speech at IV, ii, 43–77 with its sources. There are occasional lapses in the play into awkwardness and obscurity, but neither haste nor carelessness could extinguish Middleton's vivid power.

O N April 15, 1624 the impeachment of Middlesex before the House of Lords began, and when, on May 13, sentence was delivered against him, his fall was complete. It must have been during the ensuing few weeks that *A Game at Chesse*, which Middleton may already have been working on, was finished, for by June 12 it had been accepted by the King's Men, and licensed by Sir Henry Herbert, the Master of the Revels.[1] Nevertheless, the play was not performed till two months later; whether there were delays, or whether this was the normal time taken for the production and rehearsing of a new play, it is impossible to be certain. The first performance was given on Friday,[2] August 6, and immediately it created a sensation. George Lowe, writing on the evening after the second performance, said that the general opinion was that "it will be called in and the parties punished." For the moment, however, it was the blind eye of authority that was turned towards the players, who lost no time in making as large a harvest as they could. The title-page of two of the quartos states that the play "was Acted nine days to gether at the Globe on the banks side," and this is certainly the first recorded "run" in the history of the English theatre, for, as Henslowe testifies, it was the usual practice to have a different play from the company's repertoire each day, and no other series of consecutive performances is heard of until after the Restoration. The theatre was crowded to suffocation for each performance, and large numbers had to be refused admission. Chamberlain, in one of his letters to Sir Dudley Carleton, describes how the people flocked to the Globe:

The play hath been followed with extraordinarie concourse,

---

[1] For the authorities for this section, see Appendix A, *Documents relating to A Game at Chesse.*

[2] The days of the week here given have been ascertained with the aid of the "period" calendar described by Dr R. B. McKerrow in *R.E.S.* vol. 1, no. iv (Oct. 1925), p. 3 of cover.

and frequented by all sorts of people old and younge, rich and poore, masters and servants, papists and puritans, wise men etc. churchmen and statesmen...and a world besides; the Lady Smith would have gon if she could have persuaded me to go with her, I am not so sowre or severe but that I wold willingly have attended her, but that I could not sit so long, for we must have ben there before one o'clocke at farthest to find any roome.

Doubtless the company took advantage of their success to raise the prices of admission, for the writer of the note in a copy of the play in the Dyce Collection states that he had heard from some of the actors that they took fifteen hundred pounds. Critics have doubted this statement, considering the sum impossibly high, but there can be no doubt that the receipts must have eclipsed all records, for while the play was still being performed Sir Francis Nethersole wrote that "the players have gotten 100^{li} the day, knowing that ther time cannot be long."

Even as Nethersole was writing this letter, another letter was on its way from the Court at Rufford to the Lords of the Council commanding the suppression of the play. The last performance (if we allow for two Sundays on which there was no performance) was on Monday, August 16; on the 17th the theatre was closed by order of the Council, and the actors were forbidden to play. Their technical offence was that they had disobeyed the order forbidding the representation of any modern Christian king upon the stage, and the King's action in ordering steps to be taken against them was undoubtedly due to the protest made to him by the Spanish Ambassador. It is difficult to believe the statement in Conway's letter to the Lords of the Council that the Court had heard nothing of the play until the Spanish Ambassador brought it under the notice of the King, nor is there likely to be any truth in Chamberlain's hint that *A Game at Chesse* was suppressed at the instigation of Buckingham, although it is true that the references to Buckingham's fear of fatness and fondness for women in v, iii are no briefer than the passage that is omitted in most of the quartos of *Eastward Ho*. If Buckingham had cherished any animosity against the author and the actors, it is hardly likely that they would have got off so lightly.

The players appeared before the Council on August 18; but the author, who should have accompanied them, did not appear. Perhaps he too had been conscious that his time would not be long, and, not being under the necessity of appearing daily on the stage as the actors were, had decided to enjoy the success of his play from a safe distance. The actors defended themselves firmly before the Council. They produced the prompt-copy of the play; pointing to Sir Henry Herbert's allowance on the last page, they protested that it had been duly licensed by the Master of the Revels, and that they had altered or added nothing in the course of performance. The Lords of the Council assumed an expression of severity, for there was no doubt that the King's Men had been guilty of representing modern sovereigns on the stage. Accordingly, the actors were forbidden to play *A Game at Chesse*, and the Globe was to be closed until the King's further pleasure should be known A warrant was issued for Middleton's arrest, the actors gave bonds for £300 for their further appearance, and the prompt-copy was sent to the King so that he might read it and decide what further punishment might be necessary. But the actors were not without friends at Court; they were the servants of the King, and the best company performing at the time; moreover, the Earl of Pembroke, the Lord Chamberlain, who now came to their aid, had shown himself ready at other times to help them.[1] Through him, it seems, they presented a petition to James who, having vindicated his "tender regard" for the King of Spain's honour, was no longer disposed to be severe. The Council was requested to find out "by whose direction and

[1] Shakespeare, ed. Boswell and Malone, vol. III, pp. 160–161 and *Shakespeare's First Folio* by J. Compton Rhodes (1923), pp. 44–5.

application the personating of Gondomar and others was done"; that one person was to be punished severely, but, for the rest, since the King was "unwillinge for one's sake, and only fault to punish the innocent or utterly to ruine the Companie," the actors were allowed to resume their profession after giving surety never to act *A Game at Chesse* again.

If all the responsibility for the play were to be cast on to any single person, it was necessary to see what the author had to say to excuse himself, and the Privy Council turned its attention to him. He was still in hiding, but his son Edward, a young man of about twenty, was found and brought before the Board.[1] He, apparently, could give no satisfactory information but he was ordered to come up again if called upon, and probably the matter was allowed to drop there, for if the responsibility for the performance was to be cast on any one man, Sir Henry Herbert was clearly to blame for having licensed it. There is nothing to show whether he got into trouble over the incident, but if James had ever felt any real anger, it seems to have cooled down in a remarkably short space of time. The annotator of the quarto in the Dyce Collection had heard that Middleton suffered imprisonment, but he also states that some of the principal actors shared his confinement—a statement that is certainly untrue. Even if Middleton had eventually been arrested and taken to prison, the story of

---

[1] Can the "Robert Goffe, one of the Messengers of his Majesty's Chamber," who arrested Edward Middleton, have formerly been one of the King's Men? The Robert Gough who appears among "The Names of the Principall Actors in all these Playes" prefixed to the Shakespeare First Folio is probably the R. Go. who, as a boy, took the part of Aspatia in *The Second Part of the Seven Deadly Sins* for Lord Strange's Men *c.* 1590 (Greg, *Henslowe Papers*, pp. 131–132 and 152). His name is not of frequent occurrence in the actors' lists, but he is known to have taken part in *The Second Maiden's Tragedy* (1611) and *Sir John van Olden Barnavelt* (1619). His name, however, is not in the list of members of the King's Men who made their submission to Herbert on December 20, 1624. Gough died in February, 1624–5. On the other hand, the Robert Gough who made the arrest was sworn in as "one of the 40 messengers in the place of Thomas Roberts" in October, 1621 (Petyt MS. no. 515.7 in the Library of the Inner Temple).

his release by means of a riming petition is only another proof that the King was never seriously offended.

There are several echoes of the sensation caused by *A Game at Chesse* in contemporary plays. The prologue to Fletcher's *Rule a Wife and Have a Wife* contains a reference to the troubles in which the actors had recently been involved, and an apology couched in terms intended to placate the offended ears of authority:

> Do not your looks let fall,
> Nor to remembrance our late errors call,
> Because this day w'are *Spaniards* all again
> The story of our Play, and our Scene, *Spain*:
> The errors, too, do not for this cause hate;
> Now we present their wit, and not their state.

Jonson's *Staple of News* (produced in February or March, 1626)[1] also contains a satiric reference to the play, from which it appears that the actor who took the part of the Fat Bishop had died in the interim:[2]

> *Lick.* Have you no news of the stage?
> They'll ask me about new plays at dinner-time,
> And I should be as dumb as a fish.
> *Tho.* O, yes.
> There is a legacy left to the King's players
> Both for their various shifting of their scene,
> And dexterous change of their persons to all shapes,
> And all disguises, by the right reverend
> Archbishop of Spalato.
> *Lick.* He is dead
> That play'd him.
> *Tho.* Then he has lost his share of the legacy.

---

[1] *Ben Jonson*, ed. Simpson and Herford, vol. II, p. 169.

[2] Can he have been John Underwood, who died between October 10, 1624 (when he added a codicil to his will) and February 1, 1624–5 (when his will was proved)? His will is printed in the Boswell and Malone *Shakespeare*, vol. III, pp. 213–217. Underwood is mentioned in the list of "Principall Actors" in the Shakespeare Folio, and is known to have taken the part of Delio in *The Duchess of Malfi*. From his will it is clear that he was one of the more important members of the company.

> *Lick.* What news of Gondomar?
> *Tho.* A second fistula
> Or an excoriation, at the least,
> For putting the poor English play, was writ of him,
> To such a sordid use, as, is said, he did.

In Brome's *Northern Lass* (printed 1632) there is another reference; the Justice hails Squelch, who comes on disguised as a Spaniard, in these terms:

> You are a goodly man of outward parts, and except it were the Black Knight himself, or him with the fistula, the properest man I have seen of your Nation.[1]

In William Hemminge's *Elegy on Randolph's Finger*[2] (1630–32) there is an interesting reference to *A Game at Chesse*. The poets are represented as crowding forward on the strand beside Charon's boat and presenting their works to some Puritans newly come from Amsterdam; but these Puritans

> will none
> but what weare made by hopkinges or Tom stone.
> Thay Quakte at Johnson as by hym they passe
> because of Trebulation Holsome and Annanias,
> But Middleton thay seemd much to Adore
> fors learned Exercise gaynst Gundomore
> To whom they thus pray Can you Edifye
> our understandinges In this misterye?   (ll. 181–88)

These lines make it clear that Middleton was popular in City circles and that this play appealed to the Puritans as well as to the ordinary theatre-goers.

Even after the Restoration the tradition of the phenomenal success achieved by *A Game at Chesse* for the nine days on which it was performed still lingered, and in D'Avenant's *Playhouse to be Let* (1663) the Tire-woman says:

> There's such a crowd at the door as if we had a new play of Gondomar.

[1] *The Dramatic Works of Richard Brome* (1873), vol. III, p. 100.
[2] Edited by G. C. Moore Smith, Oxford, 1923.

Stage History

Few plays have ever caused such excitement in such a brief career as this of Middleton's.[1]

[1] It has been suggested that there is a reference to *A Game at Chesse* in one of Howell's *Familiar Letters* (ed. 1645, sec. 3, p. 80) written to Sir John North from Madrid: "I am sorry to heare how other Nations do much tax the *English* of their incivility to public Ministers of State, and what ballads and pasquills, and fopperies and playes, were made against *Gondamar* for doing his Masters businesse." A reference to the arrival of the dispensation from Rome, however, means that this letter must have been written towards the end of April 1623, though it is difficult to see what play is referred to. Gardiner (*History*, vol. IV, p. vi) points out that many of Howell's letters "are mere products of the bookmaker's skill, drawn up from memory long afterwards," so possibly this is one such example.

I

MANUSCRIPTS:

ALL the manuscripts, being intended for private circulation, and not for use in the playhouse, are quarto size. No manuscript gives a text that is entirely complete.

(a) *MS. O. 2. 66 in the Library of Trinity College, Cambridge.*

This manuscript contains 106 pages. There are four blank pages at the beginning; the title-page is a simple one: "A GAME / at / CHESSE. / by T.M." The verso of the title-page is blank; the next page is occupied by the Prologue; the verso is again blank, and then follow 98 pages containing the text of the play.

The manuscript is written in the same hand throughout; it is a fluent hand, which contains forms of both the "secretary" and the newer "Roman" hand, and makes no distinction between words that would have been italicised in a printed version and the rest of the text. The speech-headings, as well as the lines without them, all begin close up against the left-hand margin, but the speeches are separated by a short stroke, about half an inch long, underneath the last line of each speech, on the left side. The play is divided into acts but not into scenes; for omissions see the textual notes.

(b) *The MS. in the Henry E. Huntington Library, San Gabriel, California,* which was formerly in the Library of the Earl of Ellesmere at Bridgewater House.

This manuscript contains 108 pages. The title-page is similar to that of the Trinity MS.: "A GAME / at / CHESSE. / by Tho: Middleton." The verso is blank; the next page, which also has the verso blank, contains the Prologue; the next 102 pages contain the text of the play, and there are two blank pages at the end.

The last page of Act III, from the MS. in the Henry E. Huntington Library, San Gabriel, California, showing the handwriting of the scribe and containing a correction by Middleton at the foot of the page.

The Texts

This manuscript is written in two different hands. The greater part of the play is in the rather stilted hand of a scribe who has never learnt the Roman hand, for he is incapable of italics, and only attempts them for a few words in the Latin speech in v, i, which he copies letter for letter because he cannot understand the Latin. The other hand is the hand of the writer of the Trinity MS.; he has written the title-page, filled in a page containing II, ii, 13–19, 48–60 and 78, which had been left blank by the scribe, and completed the manuscript by adding the second and third scenes of the last act.

The scribe has made both the speech-headings and the lines without them begin beside the margins in the same way as they do in the Trinity MS., and he has also inserted the short strokes to divide the speeches. Strokes have been added in another ink so as to enclose the speech-headings in an oblong. There are a number of corrections, the majority of which are in the scribe's hand, though two corrections of the scribe's writing are certainly in the hand of the Trinity MS. These occur at the beginning of III, i, where *Enter fat Bishop* is altered to *The Fat Bishop*, and at the beginning of IV, i, where *in cipit Quartus* is altered to *Incipit Quartus*. There seem also to be several other corrections, possibly in another hand, in the same ink that added the lines to enclose the speech-headings. The text is divided into acts, but not into scenes, except that the last scene is headed *Scæna Vltima*.

(c) *MS. Lansdowne* 690, *in the British Museum.*

This manuscript and the following one have been carefully described by Mr F. P. Wilson in his important article: *Ralph Crane, Scrivener to the King's Players* in *The Library* (4th series, September 1926, pp. 194–215). It contains 102 pages of text; the title-page is divided into three compartments: in the top one is the date "1624", in the middle one the title, "A / GAME / att / Chesse", in the lowest "By Tho. Middleton", and the whole is surrounded by a border of corkscrew scrolls in ink. The manuscript is in a handwriting which Mr Wilson has identified with that of Ralph Crane, a professional scrivener, who also transcribed Middleton's *Witch* and the "Song in seuerall parts" (performed at an Easter feast given in 1622 by the Lord Mayor, Edward Barkham) as well as some important dramatic manuscripts by other authors. Crane was a skilful penman, and his calligraphy was excelled only by that of the transcriber of *The Second Maiden's Tragedy*; his Roman hand is particularly good, and he was fond of using italics wherever possible. The speech-headings have a margin to themselves further to the left than the beginnings of the lines, and they are always in italics. In the Lansdowne MS. the Prologue is inserted between the Induction and the beginning of Act I, and the text is, like all Crane's other dramatic transcripts, divided into acts and scenes.

(*d*) *MS. Malone 25, in the Bodleian Library, Oxford.*

This manuscript, which is also in Crane's handwriting, seems formerly to have belonged to John Pepys, probably the brother of Richard Pepys, the Lord Chief Justice. It was sold in the sixties of the last century by the bookseller C. J. Stewart, who, in advertising it, described it as "the original draught of the work." After four blank pages, there is a title-page very like that of the Lansdowne MS., with the same three compartments for date, title, and author's name, and similar scrolls surrounding them all. There is a blank verso, and on the next page some verses in a different hand, which indicate that the volume was a New Year's gift to Mr William Hammond (see Facsimile). The verses are signed "A Seruant to youre / Vertues, / T. M.", and there seems to be no reason to doubt that this is Middleton's own hand. The Prologue is omitted, and the Induction begins on the next sheet, which is numbered page 1, and the text of the play occupies pp. 1–69. A page from this manuscript and another from the Lansdowne MS. are reproduced in Mr F. P. Wilson's article (*op. cit.*).

The Texts

The Malone MS. lacks 770 lines or parts of lines[1] that are found in the full text, but this is not, as Stewart thought, due to the fact that it is the original draft. The broken lines and Alexandrines, which sometimes occur as the result of the omission of a passage, show clearly that this text is an abridgment of the fuller version. The cuts have been made with considerable skill, and if there were no other texts one would never suspect that so many lines had been omitted. The manuscript also possesses another very interesting feature: in the main, the stage-directions are omitted, and all the entrances are massed together at the beginning of each scene. This is the only manuscript of this type known to exist, although there are several printed texts of this form, notably *The Two Gentlemen of Verona* and the Folio version of *The Merry Wives of Windsor*. However, in the Malone MS. there are, besides *Exeunt* at the ends of the scenes, a few stage-directions in the text, viz.: *he appeares Black underneath* at III, i, 296; *Ext* at III, i, 342 and 359; *Musique. The Bl. Bᵖˢ Pawne (as in an Apparition) comes richly habited* at III, iii, 56; *ext* and *Enter agen* at IV, i, 109 and 113; *An Altar discovered with Tapors on it*; *and Images about it* at V, i, 41 and *The Images moue in a Dance* at l. 48; *Wh. Qˢ P. within* at V, ii, 81, and *within* at the head of her speeches until she enters; *The Bagg opens & the Black-Side put into it* at V, iii, 198. Two scenes from MS. Malone 25 are printed in Appendix B to illustrate Crane's methods as a transcriber and to show the special features of this manuscript.

QUARTOS:

I. A / Gameᵉ at Chæss as it was Acted / nine days to gether at the Globe / on the banks side

No date or printer's name; for engraved title-page, see Facsimile.

Collation. A² B–K⁴. A1 blank; verso: "The Picture plainly explained" and "Prologue." A2 engraved

---

[1] Mr Wilson says 760, but he does not count the ten lines of the Prologue.

title-page, no date or printer's name; verso blank. B1 "The Induction." K4v. "Epilogue." The pages are not numbered; the text is divided into acts, but not into scenes.

Copies: B.M. (C. 34. 1. 23); Emmanuel College, Cambridge; Dyce.

II. (*a*) The engraved title-page is printed from the same plate as that of I. The collation is also the same; II is a page for page reprint of I.

The second edition seems to have been called for before the type used for the first had all been broken up. H1–H2v., H3v. H4, I1–I3v. and I4v. are printed from the same setting as in I.

Copies: B.M. (C. 34. d. 38); Bod. (Mal. 176); Dyce.

(*b*) A / GAME / AT / CHESSE / As it was Acted nine Dayes / together at the GLOBE on the / *Bank-side....* Printed. 1625.

Collation. A² B–K⁴. A1 blank; verso, "Prologue." A2 Title, verses explaining the picture (without any heading), "Printed. 1625."; verso blank.

A reissue of II (*a*) without the engraved title-page and different A1, A2.

Copy: U. L. C.

III. A / Game at Chesse / as / It hath bine sundrey times Acted / at / The Globe on the Banck side.

No date or printer's name; for the title-page, which is a less elaborate engraving than that of I, see Facsimile. The engraving, which has the imprint "Ghedruckt in Lydden by Ian Masse," was printed separately and pasted on to a butt left for the purpose.

Collation. A–I⁴. A1 Title-page; verso blank. A2 "Prologue", the word "Prologue" being from a wood-block in Gothic type; verso blank. A3 "The Induction": another wood-block is used for the heading here. The heading "Epilogue" is also from a wood-block.

The Texts

Pagination: 1–68. A3 is page 1, and pages 42 and 43 are wrongly numbered 32 and 33.

The text is divided into acts and scenes.

Copies: B.M. (C. 34. d. 37); Bodl. (Mal. 247).

There are innumerable minor differences between I and II, but these two quartos may be most easily distinguished by the fact that on the last page I has "White Queene" and II "Whit Queene" in the first line of the Epilogue, and at the end of it I has *FINJS* while II has *FJNIS*. On E2 a line that is in I (II, ii, 199) has dropped out in II, and two readings prove conclusively that I and not II is the earlier quarto:

	Correct reading	I	II
F2. (III, i, 192)	How dares yon pawne unpennanc't	dares you	dare you
F4v. (III, i, 364)	My pitty flam'd	My pitty stand	My pitty stands

II has corrected some of the errors of I, and added as many of its own. Both editions teem with mistakes, and are probably much the worst of all the dramatic quartos of the period.

The text of III owes nothing to I and II, as it was printed from an independent manuscript, perhaps to supply a better text. That it was printed later than I can be inferred from a comparison of the two engraved title-pages, as that of III seems to be copied from that of the earlier one. In III the group seated around the chess-board is omitted, and the figures of Spalato and Gondomar are enlarged so as to fill all the available space. The heading at the top is retained (with slight alterations) with the two inset inscriptions *The White House* and *The Black House*. Though *The Black House* is now on the right side (so as to be above Gondomar) instead of on the left, *The White House* appears over the head of the Archbishop of Spalato. The traitor-bishop is no typical representative of the White House, and the inscription would never have been placed there unless the engraver had had the earlier engraving in front of him, and was imitating it.

It is quite possible that all the quartos were printed in 1625, and that all were surreptitiously printed. The first line of the dedicatory verses in MS. Malone 25 seems to mean that no printed copies of the play were available or contemplated at that time (*i.e.* on or about January 1, 1625), while II (*b*), which may possibly have been the last to be printed, is dated 1625. Many years later, on March 15, 1654/5, *The Game att Chesse* was entered in the Stationers' Register with six other books, including Shakespeare's *Lucrece*, as having been transferred from Martha Harrison to John Stafford and William Gilbertson. This may have been the play, or it may have been a pamphlet of the same name: *The Game at Chesse: A metaphoricall discourse shewing the present estate of this kingdome...The knights signifie the High Court of Parliament, the rookes, the Cavaliers.* 1643. In any case, it is interesting to note that *A Game at Chesse* appears at the end of *The Old Law* (1656) in the list of plays given there, and that it is there correctly ascribed to its author, although his name never appeared on the title-page of any of the printed editions.

II

It has been impossible to select two pages, one from the Trinity MS. and one from the second hand of the Bridgewater-Huntington MS., to show parallels with all the more important letter-forms in the dedication page of MS. Malone 25, but from a comparison of the plates it should be sufficiently clear that all are in the same hand, and that therefore the Trinity MS. is a transcript in the handwriting of the author, and that the Bridgewater-Huntington MS. has been completed and corrected by him. The dedication page is, of course, written with conscious and elaborate care; the other two, particularly the Bridgewater-Huntington MS., were written hastily and carelessly,

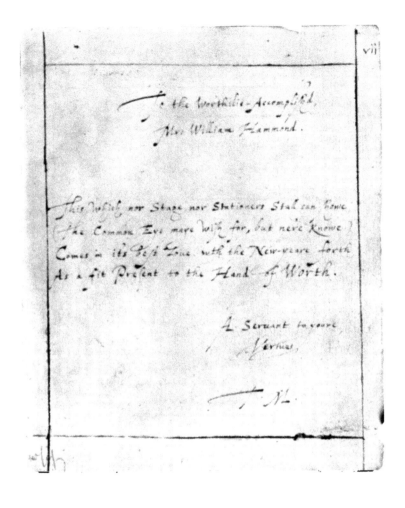

The dedication page of MS. Malone 25 in the Bodleian Library, Oxford. This page is autograph, but the rest of the MS. is in the handwriting of Ralph Crane.

though in what was doubtless Middleton's more usual hand. This is the kind of hand he was thinking of when he wrote a passage in *More Dissemblers besides Women*[1]:

> *Lac.* . . .I can write fast and fair,
> Most true orthography, and observe my stops.
> *Duch.* Stay, stay awhile,
> You do not know his hand.
> *Lac. A bastard Roman,*
> *Much like mine own*; I could go near it, madam.

The hand of the dedication page is, however, no bastard; it is the very purest Roman. Nevertheless, though the same finely-pointed pen is used in all three manuscripts, it can be seen at a glance how different the two hands may sometimes be by comparing the word *forth* at the end of the third line of the dedicatory verse with the same word in the first line of the Epilogue in the Trinity MS. For a truer comparison one must set beside the *forth* of the dedicatory page the word *for* in the fifth line of the Epilogue.

The capital letters are of most assistance in establishing the identity of the two hands. The characteristic *H* can be seen in all three plates, so too can the *A*, with its long down-stroke on the left-hand side. *E* and *M* are formed in the same way throughout: for *E* the down-stroke and lowest cross-stroke are made first, and the other cross-strokes later, and in *M* the first down-stroke is always made separately. Other features of the dedication page not illustrated in the other plates that are characteristic of the three manuscripts are the thick down-stroke in the middle of the *N*, and the extra pressure exerted on the pen at both ends of *C* and *S*. The minuscule forms are more difficult to compare; but the italic *h*, with the curl below the line, can be seen in the Epilogue. Other letters to be noticed are *k*, *l*, and the *f* with the curl at the top. Further important characteristics are the tendencies to link together *ft*, and to connect a *t* (large or small) to the

[1] Act III, sc. ii.

following letter by the cross-stroke rather than the down-stroke. One can readily believe, too, that the hand that added the flourishes to the *y*'s of the dedication page was also that which gave the similar flourishes to the *ſ*'s of the other manuscripts.

III

The texts fall into two groups: those which were transcribed by Crane (MSS. Lansdowne 690 and Malone 25) or printed from a transcription by him (Qu. III), and those which were transcribed by Middleton or copied faithfully from his papers (the Trinity and Bridgewater-Huntington MSS.) or printed from a text such as either of these (Qq. I and II).

It was first noticed while collating a copy of II with III that very often a number of the contractions in II were expanded in III; for example, where II printed *you'de* or *they're*, III had *you would* and *they are*. Out of 54 such cases observed, in 49 of them II has the contracted form and III the expanded form. Further, in 31 instances III has *hath* and *doth* where II has *has* and *does*. A careful collation of the Induction and the first act in the Trinity and Lansdowne MSS. showed that the same features were to be observed there; the Trinity MS. had *you'de*, *they're*, etc. in twelve cases, and *has* and *does* in four, where the Lansdowne MS. has *you would*, *they are*, etc. and *hath* and *doth*. Other features of the Crane transcripts are that they tend to use *it's* instead of *'tis* (Middleton never writes *it's*), and that if they contract *you would* they contract it to *you'ld* and not to *you'de*.[1]

The same test helped to show that the part of the Bridgewater-Huntington MS. in the scribe's hand could be grouped with the Trinity MS., for in each of the sixteen cases in the Induction and the first act where the other manuscripts had differed, it was found to agree with the Trinity MS. Other evidence is not wanting to show that

---

[1] See Appendix B for other examples of most of these features.

34

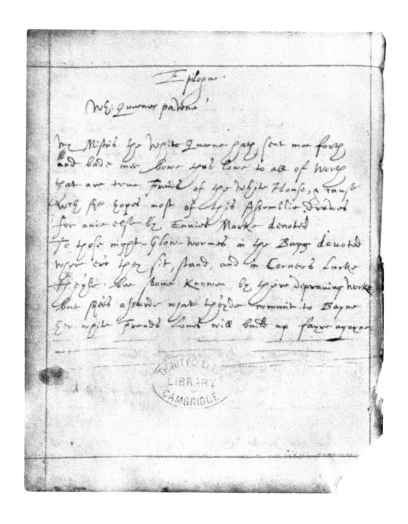

The Epilogue, from the MS. in the Library of Trinity College, Cambridge.

the scribal part of the Bridgewater-Huntington MS. is a faithful transcript of papers in Middleton's handwriting; the short strokes separating the speeches, though common in playhouse manuscripts, are probably an imitation of Middleton's practice,[1] and in some passages (*e.g.* I, i, 309–312; II, i, 169–170 and 175–176) the incorrect arrangement of the lines is exactly the same as that of the Trinity MS.[2]

There are a number of other characteristics which separate the two groups of texts. The Crane MSS. and Qu. III are divided into acts and scenes, but the other manuscripts and quartos are divided into acts only. Certain crucial stage-directions also differentiate the two groups. From the Middleton group it would appear that the rival Houses entered during the Induction to pass before Loyola, and that the Black Queen's Pawn and the White Queen's Pawn remained behind on the stage to begin the first act; in the Crane group, on the other hand, the directions explicitly state that all the characters leave the stage at the end of the Induction, and that the two pawns come on to the stage again. Another interesting divergence concerns the means by which the illusion of the apparition in III, iii was produced; in the Crane transcripts the Black Bishop's Pawn merely enters "as an Apparition richely

---

[1] It is worth noting that *Sir John van Olden Barnavelt*, Crane's one extant prompt-copy, has these strokes, but none of his other MSS. have them, and even in this one case they are far less conspicuous than those in the Trinity and Bridgewater-Huntington MSS. (see the facsimiles in Miss Frijlinck's edition of the play).

Mr C. J. Sisson, in his article: *Bibliographical Aspects of some Stuart Dramatic Manuscripts* (*R.E.S.*, October, 1925, pp. 423–427), has shown how there has been disturbance of the text in the autograph MS. of Massinger's *Beleeue as You List* such as would have led to false verse-lining if the MS. had ever gone to the printer. The reasons for false verse-lining in the Trinity MS. (in which it is fairly common) are of a different nature; where the page is not wide enough to hold the whole line, Middleton shows no hesitation in making the words crowded out begin the next line. This is the cause of a good deal of the incorrect arrangement of the lines in the Trinity MS., but in some cases there would have been room for the whole line; here it must be assumed that Middleton was copying mechanically from papers in which the last word or so had been crowded out, and did not trouble to make the correction. All the instances of false verse-lining in the Trinity MS. are recorded in the textual notes.

habited," but all the texts of the other group state definitely that he "stands before the mirror."[1] There are also a number of readings in which the Lansdowne and Malone mss. and Qu. III all agree, but disagree with the texts of the other group.[2]

The relationship of the texts within the groups is a matter not so easily settled. No manuscript gives the complete text of the play, but all the quartos do so, and therefore the copy for the quartos cannot have been derived from any one of the extant manuscripts.[3] Qq. I and II are more closely related to the Bridgewater-Huntington ms. than to the Trinity ms., as a number of readings prove,[4] although Qu. I may actually have been printed from a transcript in Middleton's handwriting, as it occasionally prints *has* as *h'as* or *ha's*, with an entirely superfluous apostrophe.[5] Middleton quite frequently writes the word in this fashion, but the scribe of the Bridgewater-Huntington ms. does not. As will be seen later, the connection between the Lansdowne and Malone mss. is a very close one, and the fact that Qu. III sometimes disagrees with them, and prefers the reading of the other group,[6] seems to show that it was

---

[1] See also the textual notes on the stage-directions at III, i, 32 and 45, 297, v, i, 1 and 40, where it will be found that L, M, and III agree in disagreeing with the other texts.

[2] *E.g.* see the textual notes on Ind. 27, 42; I, i, 41, 232, 275, 331, 332, 339, etc.

[3] If only the mss. had survived it would be an even more baffling task than it is at present to explain why one ms. lacks certain passages found in another, and *vice versa*. The known facts of the production and suppression of the play preclude any theories of alteration and revision for later performances such as critics tend to fall back upon to explain the differences between certain Shakespearian texts, such as the Second Quarto and Folio versions of *Hamlet*.

[4] See the textual notes on I, i, 5, 46, 47, 251; II, i, 184, 194; III, i, 134, 141, 160, 377; IV, i, 106; v, iii, 76.

[5] *E.g.* at II, ii, 94 and 226; IV, iv, 6 and 90.

[6] In the following Qu. III agrees with a variant reading of the Middleton group (as against that of T) with which L and M disagree: I, i, 97; II, i, 198; II, ii, 12; III, i, 90, 100, 132; IV, ii, 4, 127, 148; v, ii, 81; v, iii, 35, 67. For the cases where it agrees with the whole Middleton group, as against L and M, see the instances quoted in the next section, and in the footnotes, to prove the close relationship between L and M.

printed from a transcript made by Crane from Middleton's papers quite independently of his other two transcripts.

IV

The question now arises: If the theatrical prompt-copy of the play had been confiscated, on what materials can the numerous surviving texts have been based? This question applies with particular force to MS. Malone 25, for its form is so different from that of the ordinary dramatic texts that a special theory has been propounded by Mr Crompton Rhodes and Professor J. Dover Wilson to explain the exceptional features of texts such as this. The problem was first faced in connection with the texts of *The Two Gentlemen of Verona* and *The Merry Wives of Windsor* in the First Folio, which exhibit similar characteristics. It is suggested that if the theatrical prompt-copies were lost, the whole play still survived in the individual players' "parts," which gave all the speeches of any particular character, with the necessary cues. These parts were "assembled"; that is, the scenes were put together from the sheets containing the speeches for each separate character, and the table of entrances at the head of the scene was supplied from the "plot," or synopsis of entrances, which was hung up near the tiring-room to show the actors when they had to come on to the stage. In other words, the massed stage-directions at the head of the scene represent a transcript of the "plot," and the text an "assembling" of the different players' parts. There were, it is alleged, no stage-directions in the "parts," and therefore they had to be sought in the "plot," where they were given *en masse*, and they were accordingly copied out at the head of the scene just as the transcriber found them.[1]

[1] This, it seems to me, is the fundamental fallacy of the assembled-text theory. In the one extant "part"—Alleyn's part of Orlando in *Orlando Furioso*—the stage-directions are given in full, *as one would expect*, for the guidance of the actor in learning his part and rehearsing it. Professor Dover Wilson in his paper *The Task of Hemminge and Condell*, in the collection of essays entitled *Studies in the First Folio*, p. 73 n., faces this fact; his theory, he says, "involves the assumption that the Chamberlain's Men made out their

But, supposing that the prompt-copy of a play has been lost, there was material of another kind that was available for the transcriber which has to be taken into account. Dr Greg has drawn attention to the manuscript of *Bonduca* in the British Museum (MS. Addit. 36758).[1] This is a private transcript made by the prompter and "book-keeper" of the King's Men, and two scenes and a portion of a third are missing, and the transcriber gives from memory a synopsis of the missing portions,[2] explaining that "the occasion, why these are wanting here, [is that] the booke where by it was first Acted from is lost: and this hath beene transcrib'd from the fowle papers of the Authors w^{c}h were found." Another interesting example of the same kind is to be seen in the manuscript of *The Faithful Friends* in the Dyce Collection; here the text of IV, v was missing, and the transcriber wrote out a summary of the scene, but subsequently the missing sheet was found and was inserted opposite the transcriber's summary[3]. That loose papers in the handwriting of the author have to be reckoned with in explaining the origin of the texts of *A Game at Chesse* is proved conclusively by the Bridgewater-Huntington MS., and the presumption is that these were "foul papers" such as were relied on for the transcripts of *Bonduca* and *The Faithful Friends*. At II, ii, l. 13 the scribe found that there was a gap in the papers that he was transcribing; he left a page blank and began the next page where his papers

'parts' on a system slightly different from that adopted by the Admiral's Men"—but it is just this assumption, it seems to me, that he has no right to make. In any case, the part of Orlando gives implicit information as to the comings and goings of Orlando, and so (*mutatis mutandis*) of all the other "parts." An intelligent transcriber, such as Crane, should therefore have had no difficulty in producing a text in the ordinary form from such materials with the aid of the "plot."

[1] In his important article *Prompt Copies, Private Transcripts, and 'the Playhouse Scrivener,'* in *The Library*, September, 1925, pp. 148–156.

[2] His memory was at fault. Why (if "assembling" was a recognised process) did he not turn to the "plot" and the "parts" to fill in the gap, for he would certainly have had access to them if they still remained in the possession of the company?

[3] But see E. H. C. Oliphant: *The Plays of Beaumont and Fletcher* (1927), pp. 360–362 and 526–533.

A page from the MS. in the Henry E. Huntington Library, San Gabriel, California. The first five words are in the handwriting of the scribe, and the rest of the page in Middleton's.

went on. But what he copied out there was the beginning of III, i, and a quarto page could not possibly contain the 250 lines he had left out. Accordingly, when Middleton was looking over and completing the manuscript, he tried deftly to bridge over the gap by adding a few of the following lines (ll. 13–19 and 48–60), altered the stage-direction *Enter fat Bishop* at the beginning of III, i to a speech-heading, and inserted l. 78 between ll. 56 and 57 in order to make the events of III, i comprehensible. It could not be helped that the episode of the White Queen's Pawn's condemnation had to be omitted, and that her release later on would seem rather motiveless; Middleton had done the best he could to re-establish continuity in the book without having to insert any extra leaves.

At the first glance it might seem that the condition of MS. Malone 25 could not be more satisfactorily explained than by the theory of "assembled texts." It is known that the actors had lost their prompt-copy, and the omissions in the text would be due to the fact that the "cuts" for performance had been made before the players' parts were transcribed, and that therefore, when the assembling was undertaken, the abbreviated version only was available. Indeed Professor Dover Wilson might even be inclined to see the process of assembling somewhere at the back of the Trinity MS., for the two letters in II, i and III, i and the oration and song in v, i present features closely analogous to those of the letters, scrolls and songs in *The Merchant of Venice*, in which he finds evidence that points to "assembling" at some stage in the history of the text.[1] These four passages are headed respectively "The Letter," "The Oration" and "Song," and are without any speech-headings, even in the case of the letter in III, i, where the reading of it is interrupted by the Black Knight, and beside the song is the stage-direction: *Musique, an Altar discouerd and Statues, wth a Song.* Now it is true, as Professor Dover

[1] *The Merchant of Venice*, ed. Sir A. Quiller-Couch and J. Dover Wilson, pp. 96–99.

Wilson points out, that such passages as these, which could be read out on the stage,[1] or sung off stage, were copied out separately and not learnt by heart by the actors with the rest of their parts, and a scribe copying out the manuscript sometimes does no more than indicate such a passage,[2] as, of course, the prompter's aid would not be needed here. But it seems quite probable that an author might acquire the habit of distinguishing such portions of the play from the rest[3] (so that they could be transcribed separately) by marking them with a heading, such as "The Letter," "The Oration," etc., and it is notable that, although the letter in III, i, which is broken into by an interruption, has no speech-heading, its text has a different margin from that of the surrounding speeches, and begins a new line after the interruption.

The existence of the "foul papers" explains the fuller versions of all the manuscripts except the Malone one. It is possible to suppose that all the manuscripts may have been written before the quartos were printed, and the fact that the Malone MS. can be definitely assigned to a period shortly after the production of the play does not necessarily give it priority over the others; indeed, the condition of the Bridgewater-Huntington MS. seems to show that it was the earliest. It must be remembered, too, that MS. Malone 25 was written by Crane to Middleton's order, and any materials at Middleton's disposal would have been at hand for Crane to use, as the Lansdowne MS. and Qu. III seem to show. Furthermore, a number of important readings indicate that there is a very close relationship between the Lansdowne MS. and MS. Malone 25.

---

[1] On a blank page (f. 29v.) at the end of the autograph MS. of Massinger's *Beleeue as You List* (B.M., MS. Eg. 2828) which was used as the prompt-copy, there is a list of the letters and scrolls which were to be used in this way as "properties," with the names of the actors who used them.

[2] Cf. (for songs) the stage-directions showing where the songs from *The Witch* were inserted in *Macbeth*; similarly, the MS. of *The Faithful Friends* gives only the opening lines of the song at the end of Act I, sc. ii.

[3] Professor Dover Wilson considers this "not at all likely": *Merchant of Venice*, p. 97.

The Texts

The Malone MS. cannot have been copied from the Lansdowne MS., as it contains two lines (II, ii, 23–24) which the Lansdowne MS. lacks, but the evidence suggests that both were copied from the same source, perhaps an intermediate transcript by Crane. At IV, i, 50–54 the Trinity MS. reads:

> *Wh. Qs. p.* The time, you see,
> Is not yet come.
> *Bl. Qs. p.* But 'tis in our power now
> To bring time neerer—Knowledge is a Mastrie—
> And make it obserue us, and not wee it.

By omitting l. 53, and reading:

> *Bl. Qs. p.* But 'tis in our power now
> To make it observe us, and not we it,

the Malone MS. slightly alters the sense, which, as a rule, its omissions never do, and it is interesting to find exactly the same omission in the Lansdowne MS. At II, i, 231 these are the only two texts that read "*Anglica,* most of these are bawdie Epistles" instead of "Hah! by this hand, most of these...," and at II, ii, 68–69 they have:

> for the Phisick he prescribed
> And the base Surgeon he provided for me

where all the other texts have:

> for the phisick hee prouided
> And the base Surgeon hee inuented for mee.

A number of other similar examples might be cited,[1] but it must suffice to draw attention to two readings in IV, ii. At l. 94 most of the texts have *killing* six times, although in the Bridgewater-Huntington MS. the word is repeated seven times; here, however, the Lansdowne MS. has: *killing, killing, killing, etc.,* and the Malone MS. merely has: *killing, killing, killing*; at l. 104 all the other texts read "thirtie three pounds," which is clearly the right reading (for, as

---

[1] See the textual notes on II, i, 151; II, ii, 127; III, i, 33; III, iii, 56; IV, 1, 41 and 171; IV, ii, 105; V, i, 1; V, iii, 43.

the Black Knight says, the sum is "paid all in threes"), but these two manuscripts have "thirteene pounds." It is also worth remarking that in v, i the Lansdowne MS. has the following stage-direction at the beginning of the scene: *Enter y*ᵉ *Black-Knight (in his Litto*ʳ*) and y*ᵉ *Black-Bs Pawne (above)*, and at l. 9 this: *Enter y*ᵉ *Black House, meeting y*ᵉ *White-K*ᵗ *& Duke.* These directions do not agree exactly with those of any of the other texts, but the massed stage-direction at the head of Act v in the Malone MS. is nothing more than a combination of these two: *The Black-Knight (in his Litter) & ye Bl: B*ᵖˢ *Pawne aboue: Then y*ᵉ *Black-house, (meeting the white Knight, and white Duke.*

The close relationship existing between these two texts, although one of them is drastically abbreviated and in an unusual form, compels the abandonment of the "assembled-text" theory. One can only suggest that the cuts found in MS. Malone 25 were made, with Middleton's consent, at a time when there was a demand for copies of the play, and it was easier and more profitable to multiply it in the abbreviated form. The massing of the stage-directions at the head of each scene must be explained as an occasional idiosyncrasy of Crane's,[1] possibly copied from Ben Jonson's neo-classical habit of putting at the head of the scene the names of all the characters who appeared in it. The stage-directions in the text of MS. Malone 25, which have been already noted, are some of them descriptive and meant for a reader,[2] and not such as are likely to have been found in any of the individual player's "parts," or in the "plot." It is perhaps worth noting, too, that, although Professor A. W. Pollard's category of "literary" stage-directions cannot in the main

---

[1] Crane was adaptable in his methods, *e.g.* the strokes between the speeches in *Sir John van Olden Barnavelt*, which are not found in any of his other transcripts. His use of italics also is somewhat more restrained than usual in that play. As our knowledge of Crane's methods as a transcriber increases it may eventually be possible to decide whether he transcribed any or all of the so-called "assembled" texts in the First Folio. That he did so is by no means outside the bounds of possibility.

[2] Especially those at III, i, 296; v, i, 41 and v, iii, 198.

be defended,[1] the direction at III, iii, 56: *The Bl. B^ps Pawne (as in an Apparition)* comes *richely habited,* seems to have a literary air, as though Crane were consciously trying to avoid expressing himself in the terms of the theatre.

[1] The elaborate stage-directions in the MS. of *The Second Maiden's Tragedy,* as "literary" as any found in the drama of the period, are in a prompt-copy. A number of directions of an explanatory character are due, I think, to the fact that the author inserted them for the aid of the stage-manager when he was first reading over the play with a view to production.

A GAME AT CHESSE

The text given here is printed from a transcript of the manuscript in the Library of Trinity College, Cambridge, and its omissions have been supplied, wherever possible, from the Bridgewater-Huntington manuscript. Middleton's spelling has been preserved, but his long *I* is reproduced as *I* or *J* according to the circumstances, and, in accordance with the practice of both the Jacobean and modern printers, I have made each line begin with a capital letter. Within the line, it has sometimes been difficult to distinguish between the majuscule and minuscule forms of the letters, but it is hoped that the capitals represent Middleton's intentions fairly faithfully. Speech-headings (which have also been normalised) and stage-directions have been italicised, and the faulty arrangement of lines has been corrected. The punctuation is, in the main, left intact, though it is admittedly very careless; however, the sign ✓ has been altered to a question-mark or an exclamation-mark in accordance with modern practice, and the apostrophe is omitted where it does not actually mark a contraction (*e.g.* Middleton frequently writes *h'as*, which is only occasionally a contraction for *he has*).

Title-page of Quartos I and II (a), from a copy in the British Museum
(c. 34. d. 38).

The PICTURE *plainly explained after the manner of the* CHESSE-PLAYE

A Game at Chesse is here displayde,
Betweene the *Black* and *White House* made,
Wherein Crowne-thirsting Policy,
For the *Blacke-House* (by Falacy)
To the White-Knight, checke, often giues,   *5*
And to some straites, him thereby driues;
The *Fat-Blacke-Bishop* helps also
With faithlesse heart to giue the blow:
Yet (maugre all their craft) at length
The *White-Knight*, with wit-wondrous strength,   *10*
And circumspectiue Prudency,
Giues Check-mate by Discouery
To the *Blacke Knight*; and so at last
The game (thus) won, the *Blacke-House* cast
Into the Bagge, and therein shut,   *15*
Finde all their plumes and Cockes-combes cut.
   Plaine-dealing (thus) by wisedomes guide,
   Defeats the cheats of Craft and Pride.

To the Worthilie-Accomplish'd,
Mr: *William Hammond.*

This, Which nor Stage, nor Stationers Stall can Showe,
(The Common Eye maye wish for, but ne're knowe)
Comes in it's best loue with the New-yeare forth,
As a fit Present to the Hand of Worth.

A Seruant to youre

Vertues,

T. M.

PROLOGUE

(· . ·)

What of the Game cald Chesseplaye can bee made
To make a Stage-playe shall this daye bee playde,
First you shall see the Men in order set
States and theire pawnes, when both the Sides are met;
The houses well distinguish't, in the Game   *5*
Some men entrapt and taken, to theire shame,
Rewarded by theire playe and In the close
You shall see Check-Mate giuen, to Vertues Foes;
But the fayrst Jewell that our Hopes can deck,
Is so to playe our Game to auoyde youre Check.   *10*

The Induction!

$(\cdot.\cdot)$

Ignatius Loyola appearing, Error
at his foote as asleepe.

Ign. Hah! where! what Angle of the World is this?
That I can neyther see the politick face
Nor wth my refinde Nostrills taste the Footesteps
Of anie of my disciples, Sonnes and heyres
As well of my designes as Institution,   5
I thought theyde spread ouer the World by this time
Couerd the Earths face and made darke the Land
Like the Ægiptian Grassehoppers;
Here's too much light appeares shot from the Eyes
Of truth and goodnes neuer yet deflowrde,   10
Sure they were neuer here, then is theire Monarchie
Vnperfect yet, a iust reward I see
For theire Ingratitude so long to mee
Theire father and theire Founder,
Tis not 5 yeares since I was Saynted by 'em,   15
Where slept my honor all the time before
Could they bee so forgetfull to canonize
Theire prosperous Institutor, when they had Saynted mee
They found no roome in all theire Kalendar
To place my name that should haue remooude princes   20
Pulde the most eminent prelates by the rootes up
For my deere coming to make waye for mee,
Lett euerie pettie Martir, and St Homilie,
Roch, Main, and petronell, Itch and ague—Curers
Youre Abbesse Aldegund, and Cunigund   25
The widdowe Marcell, parson Policarpe
Sislie and Vrslie, all take place of mee,
And but for the Bissextill, or leape-Yeare
And thats but one in three, I fall by chance

51   4-2

30 Into the nine and twentieth daye of Februarie
There were no Roome else for mee, see theire loue
Theire Conscience too, to thrust mee a lame souldier
Into leape yeare, my Wraths up, and mee thinkes
I could wth the first Sillable of my name
35 Blowe up theire Colledges, up, Error, wake
Father of Supererogation, rize,
It is Ignatius calls thee, Loyola!
    Er. What haue you donne, oh I could sleepe in ignorance
Immortallie, the slumber is so pleasing,
40 I sawe the brauest setting for a Game now
That euer my eye fixt on;
    Ig. Game, what Game?
    Er. The noblest Game of all, a Game at Chesse
Betwixt our side and the Whitehouse, the men sett
45 In theire iust order readie to goe to it;
    Ig. Were anie of my Sonnes placst for the Game?
    Er. Yes, and a daughter too, a secular daughter
That playes the Black Queenes pawne, hee the Bl. Bishops,
    Ig. If euer power could showe a Mastrie in thee
50 Let it appeare in this,
    Er. Tis but a dreame
A uision you must thinke
    Ig. I care not what   *Musick*
So I behold the children of my cunning   *Enter severally in*
55 And see what ranck they keepe   *order of Game,*
    Er. You haue youre wish,   *the White and*
Behold theres the full Number of the Game, *Blacke-Houses*
Kings, and theire pawnes, Queenes, Bishops, Knights & dukes,
    Ig. Dukes? theire cald Rookes by some,
60   *Er.* Corruptiuely!
Le Roc the word, Custode de la Roche
The Keeper of the Forts, in whome both Kings
Repose much Confidence, and for theire trust sake
Courage and worth, do well deserue those Titles,
65   *Ig.* The Answeres high, I see my Sonne and daughter,
    Er. Those are 2 pawnes the Bl. Q^s. and bl: Bishops

Ig. Pawnes argue but poore Spirits, & slight preferments,
Not worthie of the name of my Disciples,
If I had stood so nigh, I would haue cut
That Bishops Throate but I'de haue had his place   70
And told the Queene a loue-tale in her Eare
Would make her best pulse dance, theres no Elixir
Of brayne or Spirit amongst 'em;
      Er. Why would you haue 'em playe agaynst themselues,
Thats quite agaynst the Rule of Game, Ignatius;   75
      Ig. Push, I would rule my selfe, not obserue rule,
      Er. Why then you'de playe a Game all by youre selfe,
      Ig. I would doo anye thing to rule alone,
Tis rare to haue the world reignd in by one;
      Er. See 'em anon, and marke 'em in theire playe,   80
Obserue, as in a dance, they glide awaye,
      Ig. Oh wth what longings will this brest bee tost,
Vntill I see this Great Game wun and lost.

ACTUS PRIMI, SCÆNA PRIMA.   [I, i.]

*Enter from the Black-house, the Bl. Queenes pawne,
from the Whitehouse the white Q^s: pawne:*

Bl. Qs. p. I ne're see that face but my pittie rizes,
When I behold so cleere a Mr-peice
Of heauens Art, wrought out of dust and Ashes,
And at next thought to giue her lost æternallie,
(In being not ours but the Daughter of heresie)   5
My soule bleedes at mine eyes;
      Wh. Qs. p. Where should Truth speake
If not in such a sorrowe? they're teares playnelie,
Beshrewe mee if shee weepe not heartilie,
What is my peace to her to take such paynes in't,   10
If I wander to losse and wth broad Eyes
Yet misse the path shee can run blindefold in,
(Through often exercize) why should my ouersight
Though in the best Game that e're Christian lost

15 Rayse the least Spring of pittie in her Eye,
Tis doubtlesse a great charitie, and no Vertue
Could win me surer;
   Bl. Qs. p. Blessed things præuayle wth't,
If euer Goodnes made a gratious promise
20 It is in yonder looke, what litle paynes
Would build a Fort for Vertue to all memorie
In that sweete Creature were the Ground-worke firmer,
   Wh. Qs. p. It has beene all my glorie to bee firme
In what I haue profest,
25   *Bl. Qs. p.* That is the Enimie
That steales youre strenght awaye, and fights agaynst you,
Disarmes youre Soule e'en in the heate of battayle,
Your Firmnes that waye makes you more infirme
For the right Christian Conflict, there I spied
30 A zealous primatiue Sparckle, but now flewe
From youre deuoted Eye,
Able to blowe up All the heresies
That euer sate in Councell wth youre Spirit
                   Enter the Bl. Bs. p:
                   a Jesuite
And here comes hee whose Sanctimonious breath
35 Can make that Sparke a Flame, list to him, Virgin,
At whose first Entrance, Princes will fall prostrate,
Weomen are weaker Vessells,
   Wh. Qs. p. By my pœnitence
A comly præsentation, and the habit,
40 To admiration reuerend,
   Bl. Qs. p. But the heart, the heart, ladie,
So meeke, that as you see good charitie picturde still
Wth yong Ones in her Armes, so will hee cherish
All his yong Tractable sweete obedient daughters
45 E'en in his bosome, in his owne deare bosome;
I am my selfe a Secular Jesuite
As manye ladies are of wealth and Greatnes,
A second sort are Jesuites in Voto,
Giuing theire Vowe in to the Father Generall

That's the black Bishop of our house, whose pawne   *50*
This Gentleman now stands for, to receiue
The Colledge habit at his holie pleasure
　　Wh. Qs. p. But how are those in Voto employde, Ladie
Till they receiue the habit,
　　Bl. Qs. p. They're not idle,   *55*
Hee findes 'em all true Labourers in the Worke
Of the Vniuersall Monarchie, wch hee
And his Disciples principallie ayme at,
Those are mayntaynde in manie Courts and palaces,
And are inducst by noble personages   *60*
Into great princes Seruices, and prooue
Some Counsellors of State, some Secretaries
All seruing in Notes of Intelligence,
(As parish clearkes theire mortuarie Bills)
To the Father Generall, so are designes   *65*
Oft times præuented, and Important Secretts
Of State discouerd, yet no Author found
But those suspected oft that are most sound,
This Mysterie is too deepe yet for youre Entrance
And I offend to sett youre Zeale so back,   *70*
Checkt by obedience wth desire to hasten
Youre progresse to perfection, I commit you
To the great workers hands, to whose graue worth
I fitt my Reuerence, as to you my wishes.
　　Bl. Bs. p. Do'st finde her supple?
　　Bl. Qs. p. There's a litle passage made;   *75*
　　Bl. Bs. p. Let mee contemplate
Wth holie wonder season my Accesse,
And by degrees approach the Sanctuarie
Of unmacht bewtie sett in grace and Goodnes,   *80*
Amongst the Daughters of men I haue not found
A more catholicall Aspect, that Eye
Do's promise single life and meeke obedience
Uppon those lips the sweete fresh Buds of youth,
The holie Dewe of prayer lyes like pearle   *85*
Dropt from the opening Eye-lids of the Morne

Uppon the bashfull Rose; how bewteouslie
A gentle Fast not rigorouslie imposde
Would looke uppon that cheeke, and how delightfully
90 The curteous phisick of a tender pennance
Whose Vtmost Crueltie should not exceede
The first feare of a Bride to beate downe frayltie
Would worke to sound health youre long festerd Judgm̄t,
And make youre Merit, wch through erring Ignorance
95 Appeares but spotted Righteousnes to mee
Far cleerer then the Innocence of Infants:
    Wh. Qs. p. To that good worke I bowe, and will become
Obedience humblest daughter, since I finde
Th' assistance of a sacred Strenght to ayde mee
100 The labour is as easie to serue Vertue
The right waye, since tis shee I euer serude
In my desire, though I transgrest in Judgment:
    Bl. Bs. p. Thats easilie absolud amongst the rest,
You shall not finde the Vertue that you serue now
105 A sharpe and cruell Mistris, her Eare's open
To all youre Supplications, you maye boldlie
And safelie let in the most secret Sin
Into her knowledge, wch like uanish't man
Neuer returnes into the world agen,
110 Fate locks not up more trulier.
    Wh. Qs. p. To the Guiltie
That maye appeare some benefit,
    Bl. Bs. p. Who is so Innocent
That neuer stands in neede on't, in some kinde,
115 If euerie thought were blabd thats so confest
The uerie Ayre wee breathe would bee unblest:
Now to the worke indeed wch is to catch
Her Inclination, that's the spetiall use
Wee make of all our practise in all kingdomes,
120 For by disclosing theire most secret Fraylties
Things, wch once ours, they must not hide from us,
Thats the first article in the Creede wee teach 'em;
Finding to what poynt theire bloud most enclines,

Knowe best to apt them then to our Designes:
Daughter! the sooner you disperse youre Errors,   *125*
The sooner you make haste to youre Recouerie
You must part wth 'em, to bee nice or modest
Toward this good Action, is to imitate
The Bashfullnes of one conceals an Vlcer,
For the uncomelie parts the Tumor uexes   *130*
Til't bee past Cure, Resolue you thus far, ladie,
The priuat'st thought that runs to hide it selfe
In the most secret Corner of youre heart now
Must bee of my Acquayntance, so familiarlye
Neuer shee frend of youre Night-Councell neerer,   *135*
   Wh. Qs. p. I stand not much in feare of anie Action
Guiltie of that black time (most noble Holines)
I must confesse, as in a sacred Temple
Throngd wth an Auditorie, some come rather
To feede on humayne obiect, then to taste   *140*
Of Angells Foode;
So in the congregation of quick thoughts
Wch are more infinite then such assemblies
I cannot wth truths safetie speake for all,
Some haue beene wanderers, some fond, some sinfull,   *145*
But those found euer but poore Entertaynment
They'de small encouragement to come agen,
The single life wch stronglie I professe now,
Heauen pardon mee, I was about to part from;
   Bl. Bs. p. Then you haue past through loue?   *150*
   Wh. Qs. p. But left no Stayne
In all my passage (Sir) no print of Wrong
For the most chast Mayde that maye trace my footsteps;
   Bl. Bs. p. How came you off so cleere?
   Wh. Qs. p. I was dischargd   *155*
By an inhumayne Accident, wch modestie
Forbids mee to putt anie language to:
   Bl. Bs. p. How you forget youre selfe, all actions
Clad in theire proper language, though most sordid,
My Eare is bound by dutie, to lett in   *160*

And lock up euerlastinglie, shall I helpe you
Hee was not found to answere his Creation,
A Vestall Virgin in a Slip of prayer
Could not deliuer mans losse modestlier,
165 Twas the white Bishops pawne;
  Wh. Qs. p. The same (blest Sir)
  Bl. Bs. p. An Heretique well pickled,
  Wh. Qs. p. By base trecherie
And Violence preparde by his Competitor
170 The black knights pawne, whome I shall euer hate fort
  Bl. Bs. p. Twas of Reuenges, the unmanliest waye
That euer Riuall tooke, a Villanie
That for youre sake Ile ne're absolue him off,
  Wh. Qs. p. I wish it not so heauie,
175 *Bl. Bs. p.* Hee must feele it
I neuer yet gaue absolution
To anie Crime of that unmanning Nature;
It seemes then you refusde him for defect,
Therein you stand not pure from the desire
180 That other weomen haue in ends of marriage,
Pardon my boldnes, if I sift youre goodnes
To the last grayne;
  Wh. Qs. p. I reuerence youre paynes (Sir)
And must acknowledge custome to enioye
185 What other weomen challenge and possesse
More rulde mee then desire, for my desires
Dwell all in ignorance, and Ile neuer wish
To knowe that fond waye maye redeeme them thence,
  Bl. Bs. p. I neuer was so taken, besett doublie
190 Now wth her Judgment, what a strenght it putts forth
I bring worke neerer to you, when you haue seene
A Mr-peice of man, composde by heauen
For a Great Princes fauour, kingdomes loue,
So exact, Enuie could not finde a place
195 To stick a Blot on person or on fame;
Haue you not found Ambition swell youre wish then?
And desire steere youre Bloud?

58

Wh. Qs. p. By Vertue neuer,
I haue onelie in the dignitie of the Creature
Admirde the Makers Glorie;   *200*
  Bl. Bs. p. Shees impregnable;
A Second Seige must not fall off so tamelie,
Shee's one of those must bee informde to knowe
A daughters dutie, wch some take untaught,
Her modestie brings her behinde hand much,   *205*
My ould meanes I must flye to, yes, tis it;
Please you peruse this small Tract of obedience
Twill helpe you forward well,
  Wh. Qs. p. Sir, thats a Vertue
I haue euer thought on wth espetiall Reuerence   *210*
  Bl. Bs. p. You will conceiue by that, my power, youre dutie,
  Wh. Qs. p. The knowledge will bee pretious of both (Sir)
                                    Enter Wh: Bps. pawne
  Wh. Bs. p. What makes yond troubler of all christian Waters
So neere that blessed Spring, but that I knowe
Her Goodnes is the Rock from whence it issues   *215*
Unmoueable as Fate, twould more afflict mee
Then all my suffrings for her, wch, so long
As shee holds constant to the house shee comes of
The whitenes of the cause, the side, the Qualitie,
Are Sacrifices to her worth, and Vertue,   *220*
And though confinde, in my relligious Joyes
I marrie her and possesse her,
  Bl. Bs. p. Behold ladie,
The 2 inhumayne Enimies, the black knights pawne
And the white Bishops, the Gelder, and the Gelded,   *225*
  Wh. Qs. p. There's my greefe, my hate,   *Enter Bl. Kts.*
  Bl. Kts. p. What in the Jesuites fingers, by this hand   *pawne.*
I'le giue my part now for a parrots feather,
Shee neuer returnes Vertuous, tis impossible,
Ile undertake more wagers will bee layde   *230*
Uppon a Vserers returne from hell
Then uppon hers from him now; haue I bin guiltie
Of such base malice that my uerie Conscience

59

Shakes at the memorie of, and when I looke
235 To gather fruit finde nothing but the Sauin Tree
Too frequent in Nuns Orchards, and there planted
By all Coniecture to destroye fruite rather,
I will bee resolude now, (most noble Virgin)
   Wh. Qs. p. Ignoble Villayne! dare that unhallowed tong
240 Laye hold uppon a Sound so gratious?
Whats Noblenes to thee? or Virgin Chastitie
They're not of thy Acquayntance, talke of Violence
That shames creation, deeds would make night blush
Thats companie for thee, hast thou the Impudence
245 To court mee wth a leprosie uppon thee
Able t'infect the walls of a great Building
   Bl. Bs. p. Sonne of offence, forbeare, goe, sett youre euill
Before youre Eyes, a pœnitentiall Vesture
Would better become you, some shirt of hayre,
250   *Bl. Kts. p.* And you a 3 pound Smock, stead of an Albe
An Epicœne Cassible, this holie Fellow
Robs safe and closse, I feele a sting that's worse too,
White pawne! hast so much charitie to accept
A Reconcilement make thy owne Conditions
255 For I begin to bee extreamelie burdned
   Wh. Bs. p. No truth, or peace of that black house protested
Is to bee trusted, but for hope of quittance
And warnd by diffidence I maye entrap him soonest,
I admit conference;
260   *Bl. Kts. p.* It is a Noblenes
That makes confusion cleaue to all my meritts,
   Bl. Bs. p. That treatise will instruct you fullie:
                                        Enter Bl: Kt.
   Bl. Kt. So, so,
The Busines of the Vniuersall Monarchie
265 Goes forward well now, the great Colledge pott
That should bee alwayes boyling, wth the fuell
Of all Intelligences possible
Thorough the Christian kingdomes, is this fellowe
Our prime Incendiarie, one of those

The Count Gondomar. From an engraving of a painting by Velasquez.
(It will be noticed that the figure of Gondomar in each of the three
title-pages reproduced is derived from this engraving.)

That promist the white Kingdome 7 yeares since   *270*
To our black house? put a new daughter to him
The great worke stands, hee mindes nor Monarchie
Nor Hierarchie, (diuiner principalitye)
I'ue bragd lesse,
But haue donne more then all the Conclaue on em,   *275*
Take theire Assistant fathers in all parts,
I, or theire father Generall in to boote,
And what I haue donne, I haue donne facetiouslie,
Wth pleasant subteltie and bewitching Courtship
Abusde all my Beleiuers wth delight   *280*
They tooke a Comfort to bee coosned by mee,
To manie a Soule, I haue let in mortall poyson
Whose cheekes haue crackt wth laughter to receiue it,
I could so rowle my pills in sugred sillables
And strewe such kindlie Mirth ore all my mischiefs,   *285*
They tooke theire Bane in waye of Recreation
As pleasure steales Corruption into Youth
Hee spyes mee now, I must uphold his reuerence
Espetiallie in publick, though I knowe
Priapus, Guardian of the Cherrie Gardens   *290*
Bacchus and Venus Chit, is not more Vitious
 Bl. Bs. p. Blessings Accumulation keepe wth you (Sir,)
 Bl. Kt. Honors dissimulation bee youre due (Sir)
 Wh. Qs. p. How deepe in dutie his Obseruance plundges
His charge must needs bee reuerend,   *295*
 Bl. Bs. p. I am confessor
To this black K^t. too, you see Deuotion's fruitfull
Sh'as manye Sonnes and daughters,
 Bl. Kt. I doo this the more
T'amaze our Aduersaries to behold   *300*
The reuerence wee giue these Guitenens,
And to beget a sound opinion
Of Holines in them and Zeale in vs,
As also to enuite the like Obedience
In other Pusills, by our meeke Example,   *305*
So, is youre Trifle uanisht?

Bl. Bs. p. Trifle call you her? tis a good Pawne Sir
Sure shee's the second pawne of the white house,
And to the opening of the Game I hold her,
310   *Bl. Kt.* I you
Hold well for that I knowe youre playe of ould
If there were more Q^s: pawnes youde plye the Game
A great deale harder, (now Sir weere in priuate)
But what for the mayne worke, the great Existence
315 The Hope monarchall,
  Bl. Bs. p. It goes on in this,
  Bl. Kt. In this? I cannot see'te,
  Bl. Bs. p. You maye denye so
A dyalls motion, cause you cannot see
320 The hand moue, or a winde that rends the Cedar,
  Bl. Kt. Where stops the Current of Intelligence,
Youre father Generall Bishop of the black-house
Complaynes for want of worke;
  Bl. Bs. p. Here's from all parts
325 Sufficient to employe him, I receiude
A packet from the Assistant Fathers latelie,
Looke you theres Anglica, this Gallica
  Bl. Kt. I marrie Sir, theres some quick flesh in this
  Bl. Bs. p. Germanica!
330   *Bl. Kt.* Thinke theyue seald this wth Butter,
  Bl. Bs. p. Italica this!
  Bl. Kt. They put theire pens the Hebrewe waye methinkes
  Bl. Bs. p. Hispanica here!
  Bl. Kt. Hispanica, blinde worke tis,
335 The Jesuite has writ this wth Juice of lemmans sure
It must bee held closse to the fire of Purgatorie
Er't can bee read
  Bl. Bs. p. You will not loose youre Jest Knight
Though it wounded youre owne Fame,   *Enter wh. Ks.*
340   *Bl. Kt.* Curanda Pecuniâ;   *pawne*
  Bl. Bs. p. Take heede S^r, weere entrapt the wh. Kings
pawne!
  Bl. Kt. Hee's made our owne (man) halfe in Voto youres,

His hearts in the black house, leaue him to mee,
Most of all frends endeerde, pretiouslie spetiall;
 Wh. Ks. p. You see my outside, but you knowe my heart, K^t, *345*
Great difference in the Colour, there's some Intelligence
And as more ripens, so youre knowledge still
Shall prooue the richer, there shall nothing happen
(Beleiue it) to extenuate youre cause
Or to oppresse her frends, but I will striue   *350*
To crosse it wth my Councell, purse and power,
Keepe all Supplies back, both in meanes and men
That maye rayse agaynst you, wee must part,
I dare not longer of this theame discusse,
The Eare of State is quick and Jealous: *355*
 Bl. Kt. Excellent Estimation, thou art ualued
Aboue the Fleete of Gold, that came short home,
Poore Jesuite ridden Soule, how art thou foolde
Out of thy Fayth, from thy Alleagance drawen
Wch path so ere thou tak'st thou'rt a lost Pawne   *360*

Finit Actus primus:

ACTUS SECUNDI SCÆNA PRIMA.   [II, i.]

Enter Wh. Qs. pawne with a booke in her hand.

 Wh. Qs. p. And here agen it is the daughters dutie
To obaye her Confessors command in all things
Wthout exception, or expostulation,
 'Tis the most generall Rule that e're I read of,
Yet when I thinke how boundlesse Vertue is   *5*
Goodnes and Grace, tis gentlie reconcilde
And then it appeares well to haue the power
Of the dispenser as uncircumscribd

Enter Bl. Bs. p.

 Bl. Bs. p. Shee's hard uppon't, twas the most modest Key
That I could use to open my Intents,   *10*
What little or no paynes goes to some people,

63

Hah! a Seald Note, whence this?
To the black Bishops pawne these, how! to mee?
Strange, who subscribes it? the Black King! what would hee?

the letter

$(\,\cdot\,\cdot\,)$

15   Pawne! sufficientlie holie, but unmeasureablie politique; wee had late intelligence from our most indus-
trious Seruant famous in all parts of Europe, (our
Knight of the black house, that you haue at this instant
in chace, the white Queenes pawne, and uerie liklie
20   by the carriage of youre Game to entrap and take
her, these are therefore to require you by the burning
affection I beare to the Rape of Deuotion, that
speedilie uppon the surprizall of her, by all watch-
full aduantage you make some attempt uppon
25   the white Queenes person whose fall or prostitution
our Lust most uiolentlie rages for,

(Sir) after my desire has tooke a Julepp
For its owne Inflammation, that yet scorches mee,
I shall haue cooler time to thinke of yours:
30 Sh'as past the generall Rule, the large Extent
Of our præscriptions for obedience
And yet wth what Alacritie of Soule
Her Eye moues on the Letters;
   Wh. Qs. p. Holie Sir,
35 Too long I haue mist you, oh youre absence starues mee,
Hasten for times redemption (worthie Sir)
Laye youre commands as thick and fast uppon mee
As you can speake 'em, how I thirst to heare 'em,
Sett mee to worke uppon this spatious Vertue
40 Wch the poore Span of lifes too narrowe for
Boundlesse Obedience,
The humblest yet the mightiest of all duties;
Well here sett downe a Vniuersall Goodnes;
   Bl. Bs. p. By holines of Garment her safe Innocence

Has frighted the full meaning from it selfe,   45
Shee's farder off from understanding now
The language of my Intent then at first meeting;
   Wh. Qs. p. For Vertues sake, good sir, command me somthîg,
Make tryall of my dutie in some small seruice
And as you finde the fayth of my Obedience there,   50
Then trust it wth a greater;
   Bl. Bs. p. You speake sweetelie,
I do command you first then—
   Wh. Qs. p. Wth what ioye
I do prepare my dutie,   55
   Bl. Bs. p. To meete mee
And seale a kisse of loue uppon my Lip,
   Wh. Qs. p. Hah!
   Bl. Bs. p. At first disobedient, in so litle too,!
How shall I trust you wth a greater then,   60
Wch was youre owne request;
   Wh. Qs. p. Praye send not back
My Innocence to wound mee, bee more curteous,
I must confesse much like an ignorant plaintiffe
Who presuming on the fayre path of his meaning   65
Goes rashlie on, till on a suddayne brought
Into the wildernes of Lawe, by words
Dropt unaduisedlie, hurts his good cause
And giues his aduersarie aduantage by it
Applie it you can best (Sir) if my obedience   70
And youre command can finde no better waye
Fond men command, and wantons best obaye;
   Bl. Bs. p. If I can at that distance send you a blessing,
Is it not neerer to you in mine Armes?
It flyes from these lips dealt abroad in parcells,   75
And I to honor thee aboue all daughters
Enuite thee home to the house, where thou mayst surfet
On that, wch others miserablie pine for,
A fauour wch the daughters of great Potentates
Would look on Enuies colour but to heare,   80
   Wh. Qs. p. Goodmen maye err somtimes, you are mistaken sure,

If this bee Vertues path, tis a most strange one,
I neuer came this waye before,
   Bl. Bs. p. Thats youre ignorance,
85 And therefore shall that Ideot still conduct you
That knowes no waye but one, nor euer seekes it,
If there bee twentie wayes to some poore Village,
Tis strange that Vertue should bee put to one,
Youre feare is wondrous faultie, cast it from you
90 Twill gather else in Time a Disobedience
Too stubborne for my pardon,
   Wh. Qs. p. Haue I lockt my selfe
At unawares into Sins seruitude
Wth more desire of Goodnes? is this the Top
95 Of all strickt Order,? and the holiest
Of all societies, the 3 Vowde people
For pouertie, obedience, chastitie,
The last the most forgot, when a Virgins ruinde
I see the great worke of obedience
100 Is better then halfe finisht;
   Bl. Bs. p. What a Stranger
Are you to dutie growen, what distance keepe you?
Must I bid you come forward to a happines
Youre selfe should sue for? twas neuer so wth mee,
105 I dare not let this Stubbornes bee knowen
Twould bring such feirce hate on you, yet presume not
To make that curteous care a priuiledge
For willfull disobedience, it turnes then
Into the blacknes of a Curse uppon you,
110 Come, come, bee neerer,
   Wh. Qs. p. Neerer?
   Bl. Bs. p. Was that Scorne?
I would not haue it prooue so, for the hopes
Of the grand Monarchie, if it were like it
115 Let it not dare to stir abroad agen
A stronger Ill will coape wth't,
   Wh. Qs. p. Blesse mee, threatens mee
And quite dismayes the good strenght that should helpe mee,

66

I neuer was so doubtfull of my safetie,

   Bl. Bs. p. Twas but my Jealousie, forgiue mee Sweetnes   *120*

Yond is the house of Meeknes and no Venom liues

Under that Roofe, bee neerer, why so fearefull?

Neerer the Altar the more safe and sacred,

   Wh. Qs. p. But neerer to the offeror oft more wicked

   Bl. Bs. p. A playne and most insufferable Contempt,   *125*

My glorie I haue lost uppon this woman

In freelie offring that shee should haue kneelde

A yeare in Vayne for, my respect is darkned

Giue mee my Reuerence agen, thou hast robd mee of

In thy repulse, thou shalt not carrie it hence   *130*

   Wh. Qs. p. Sir,

   Bl. Bs. p. Thou'rt too great a Winner to depart so

And I too deepe a looser to giue waye to it,

   Wh. Qs. p. Oh heauen!

   Bl. Bs. p. Laye mee downe Reputation   *135*

Before thou stirst, thy nice Virginitie

Is recompence too litle for my Loue

Tis well if I accept of that for both

Thy losse is but thine owne, there's Art to helpe thee

And fooles to passe thee to, in my discouerie   *140*

The whole Societie suffers, and in that

The hope of Absolute Monarchie eclipst,

Assurance thou canst make none for thy Secrecie

But by thy honors losse, that Act must awe thee,

   Wh. Qs. p. Oh my distrest Condition!   *145*

   Bl. Bs. p. Do'st thou weepe?

If thou hadst anie pittie this necessitie

Would wring it from thee, I must else destroye thee

Wee must not trust the policie of Europe

Uppon a womans tongue,   *150*

   Wh. Qs. p. Then take my life sir,

And leaue my honor for my guide to heauen,

   Bl. Bs. p. Take heede I take not both, wch I haue uowde

Since if longer thou resist mee,

   Wh. Qs. p. Helpe, o helpe—   *155*

Bl. Bs. p. Art thou so cruell for an honors Bubble
To undoo a whole Fraternitie, and disperse
The secretts of most nations lockt in us;
   Wh. Qs. p. For heauen and Vertues sake;
160 *Bl. Bs. p.* Must force confound noyse?

                               a Noyse wthin

Hah! whats that? silence if fayre worth bee in thee,
   Wh. Qs. p. I uenture my Escape uppon all dangers now
   Bl. Bs. p. Who comes to take mee let mee see that Pawns face
Or his proud tympanous M^r sweld wth state wind
165 Wch being once prickt in the Conuocation house
The corrupt Ayre puffs out and hee falls shr[i]ueled,
   Wh. Qs. p. I will discouer thee Arch hipocrite
To all the kinreds of the earth   *Exit*
   Bl. Bs. p. Confusion!
170 In that Voyce rings the Alarum of my undoing
How! wch waye scapte shee from mee?   *Enter bl. Qs. P.*
   Bl. Qs. p. Are you mad?
Can lust infatuate a man so hopefull,
No patience in youre bloud, the Dogstar reignes sure
175 Time and fayre Temper would haue wrought her plyant,
I spied a pawne of the whitehouse walke neere us
And made that Noyse a purpose to giue warning
For mine owne turne, wch end in all I worke for,
   Bl. Bs. p. Mee thinkes I stand ouer a powder-Vault
180 And the Match now a kindling, whats to be donne?
   Bl. Qs. p. Aske the black Bishops councell youre his pawne
Tis his owne case, hee will defend you maynelie,
And happilie here hee comes wth the Bl. Knight too,

                         Enter Bl. Bp, and Bl.
                                 Kt.

   Bl. B. Oh y'aue made noble worke for the white house
      yonder,
185 This Act will fill the Aduersaries mouth
And blowe the Lutherans cheeke, tillt crack agen,
   Bl. Kt. This will aduance the great Monarchall busines
In all parts well, and helpe the Agents forward,

What I in 7 yeare labourd to accomplish
One Minute setts back by some Codpeice Colledge still,   *190*
   Bl. Bs. p. I dwell not, Sir, alone in this default
The black house yeilds mee partners;
   Bl. B. All more cautelous,
   Bl. Kt. Qui cautè, castè, thats my Motto euer,
I haue trauayld wth that word ouer most kingdomes   *195*
And layne safe wth most Nations, of a leaking bottome,
I haue beene as often tost on Venus Seas
As trimmer fresher Barkes, when sounder Vessells
Haue layne at Anchor, that is, kept the doore;
   Bl. B. Shee has no witnesse then!   *200*
   Bl. Bs. p. None, none
   Bl. Kt. Grosse, witnesse!
When went a man of his Societie
To mischeife wth a witnesse,
   Bl. B. I haue don't then,   *205*
Awaye, uppon the wings of Speede take posthorse
Cast thirtie leagues of Earth behind thee suddainlie
Leaue letters Antedated wth our house
Ten dayes at least from this,
   Bl. Kt. Bishop I tast thee,   *210*
Good strong Episcopall Councell, take a bottle on't
Twill serue thee all the Journey,
   Bl. Bs. p. But good Sir, how
For my getting forth, unspied?
   Bl. Kt. There's check agen,   *215*
   Bl. Qs. p. No, Ile helpe that!
   Bl. Kt. Well sayde my bouncing Jesuitesse,
   Bl. Qs. p. There lyes a secret Vault,
   Bl. Kt. Awaye, make haste then,
   Bl. Bs. p. Run for my Cabinet of Intelligences   *220*
For feare they search the house, good Bishop burne 'em rather
I cannot stand to pick 'em, now,
   Bl. B. Bee gon,
The dangers all in you
   Bl. Kt. Let mee see Queenes pawne,   *225*

How formallie h'as packt up his Intelligences,
H'as layde 'em all in Truckle beds mee thinkes,
And like Court-Harbingers has writ theire names
In Chalke uppon theire Chambers, Anglica!
230 Oh this is the English house, what newes there tro?
Hah! by this hand, most of these are bawdie Epistles
Time they were burnt indeed, whole Bundles on 'em,
Heres from his daughter Blanch, and daughter bridget
From theire safe Sanctuarie in the Whitefriers,
235 These from two tender Sisters of Compassion
In the bowells of Bloomsburie;
3 from the Nunnerie in Drurie Lane,
A fire, a fire, good Jesuitesse, a fire,
What haue you there?
240   *Bl. B.* A note Sir of State-policie
And one exceeding safe one,
   Bl. Kt. Praye letts see it sir,—
To sell awaye all the powder in a kingdome
To præuent blowing up, that's safe Ile able it,
245 Heres a facetious obseruation now,
And suites my humour better, hee writes here
Some wiues in England will committ Adulterie,
And then send to Rome for a Bull for theire housbands,
   Bl. B. Haue they those Shifts?
250   *Bl. Kt.* Oh there's no Female breathing
Sweeter and subteller, here wench take these papers
Scortch mee 'em soundlie, burne 'em to French Russet
And put 'em in agen,
   Bl. B. Why whats youre Mysterie?
255   *Bl. Kt.* Oh Sir twill mock the Aduersarie strangelye
If e're the house bee searchd, twas donne in Venice
Uppon the Jesuiticall Expulse there,
When the Inquisitors came all spectacld
To pick out Sillables out of the Dung of Treason
260 As children pick out Cherriestones, yet found none
But what they made themselues wth ends of Letters,
Doo as I bid you, pawne,

70

Marco Antonio de Dominis, Archbishop of Spalatro. From the engraved
portrait in Vol. I of his *De Republica Ecclesiastica* (1617).

Bl. Qs. p. Feare not, in all,
I loue Roguerie too well to lett it fall,
How now! what newes wth you?   *Enter Bl. Kts. pawn,* 265
  Bl. Kts. p. The Sting of Conscience
Afflicts mee so, for that inhumayne Violence
On the White Bishops pawne, it takes awaye
My Joye, my rest;
  Bl. Qs. p. This tis to make an Eunuch   270
You made a Sport on't then,
  Bl. Kts. p. Cease Aggrauation,
I come to bee absolude for't, where's my Confessor?
Why do'st thou poynt to the Ground?
  Bl. Qs. p. Cause hee went that waye,   275
Come, come helpe mee in wth this cabinet
And after I haue singd these papers throughlie
Ile tell thee a strange storie;
  Bl. Kts. p. If't bee sad
Tis welcome,   280
  Bl. Qs. p. Tis not troubled wth much mirth Sir;   *exeunt*

          Enter Fat Bishop wth a pawne.   [II, ii.]

F. B. Pawne!
  F. Bs. p. I attend at youre great holines seruice
  F. B. For great I grant you, but for greatlie holie
There the soyle alters, fatt Cathedrall Bodies
Haue uerie often but leane litle soules   5
Much like the Ladie in the lobsters head,
A great deale of Shell and Garbidge of all colours,
But the pure part that should take wings, and mount
Is at last Gaspe, as if a man should gape
And from this huge Bulke lett forth a Butterflye,   10
Like those big-bellyed Mountaynes wch the Poet
Deliuers, that are brought abed wth Mousflesh,
Are my Bookes printed, Pawne? my last Inuectiues
Agaynst the Blackhouse?
  F. Bs. p. Readie for publication,   15
For I sawe perfect Bookes this morning (Sir)

F. B. Fetch mee a fewe wch I will instantlie
Distribute 'mongst the white house;
   F. Bs. p. Wth all speede, Sir,   *exit Bs. p.*
20 *F. B.* Tis a most lordlie life to rayle at ease,
Sitt, eate, and feede uppon the Fat of one kingdome,
And rayle uppon another wth the Juice on't,
I haue writt this booke out of the strenght & marrowe,
Of 6 and 30 dishes at a meale,
25 But most on't out of Cullisse of Cock sparrowes
Twill stick and glut the faster to the Aduersarie,
Twill slit the Throat of theire most Caluish Cause
And yet I eate but litle Butchers meate
In the Conception,
30 Of all things I commend the Wh. house best
For plentie and Varietie of Victualls,
When I was one of the black Side profest
My flesh fell halfe a Cubit, time to turne
When my owne Ribs reuolted, but to saye true
35 I haue no preferment yet, that's sutable
To the greatnes of my person and my parts,
I grant I liue at ease, for I am made
The Mr: of the Beds, the long Acrë of Beds,
But there's no Marygolds that shutts and opens,
40 Flower-Gentles, Venus Bath, Apples of Loue,
Pincks, Hiacinths, Honysuckles Daffadownedillies
There was a time I had more such Drabs then Beds
Now I'ue more Beds then Drabs;
Yet there's no eminent Trader deales in Holesale
45 But shee and I haue clapt a Bergayne up
Lett in at Watergate, for wch I haue rackt
My Tennants pursestrings that they haue twangd agen;
Yonder Black Knight, the Fistula of Europe,   *Enter Bl. Kt.*
Whose disease once I undertooke to cure   *and Bl. Bp.*
50 Wth a high-holborne Halter, when hee last
Vouchsafte to peepe into my priuiledgd lodgings
Hee sawe good Store of plate there, and rich hangings,
Hee knewe I brought none to the whitehouse wth mee,

I haue not lost the use of my profession
Since I turnd whitehouse Bishop;   55

Enter his pawne wth
Bookes!

Bl. Kt. Looke more Bookes yet,
Yond greasie turnecoate Gurmundizing Prelate
Do's worke our house more mischeife by his Scripts
His Fat and fulsome Volumes,
Then the whole bodie of the aduerse partie   60
    Bl. B. Oh twere a Mr: peice of Serpent Subteltie
To fetch him a this side agen,
    Bl. Kt. And then dam him
Into the Bagg for euer, or expose him
Agaynst the aduerse party wch now hee feedes uppon   65
And that would double dam him, my reuenge
Has prompted mee alreadie, Ile confound him
A both sides for the phisick hee prouided
And the base Surgeon hee inuented for mee;
Ile tell you what a most uncatholick Jest   70
Hee putt uppon mee once, when my payne torturd mee,
Hee told mee hee had found a present Cure for mee
Wch I grewe proud on, and obserud him seriouslie,
What thinke you twas, being Execution daye
Hee showde the hangman to mee out at Windowe   75
The common hangman;
    Bl. B. Oh Insufferable!
    Bl. Kt. Ile make him the Baloom Ball of the churches
And both the sides shall tosse him, hee lookes like one,
A thing sweld up with mingled drinck and Vrine   80
And will bound well from one side to another!
Come, you shall write, our Second Bishop absent,
Wch has yet no Employment in the Game
Perhaps nor euer shall, it maye bee wun
Wthout his motion, it rests most in ours   85
Hee shall bee flatterd wth Sede Vacante
Make him beleiue hee comes into his place
And that will fetch him wth a Vengeance to us,

For I knowe powder is not more Ambitious
90 When the Match meetes it, then his minde for mounting
As couetous, and lecherous
    Bl. B. No more, now Sir,
Both the Sides fill,   *Enter both houses,*
    Wh. K. This has beene lookte for long,
95   *F. B.* The stronger sting it shootes into the Bloud
Of the Black Aduersarie, I am ashamde now
I was theirs euer, what a Lumpe was I
When I was lead in ignorance and blindnes;
I must confesse,
100 I haue all my life time playde the foole till now,
    Bl. Kt. And now hee playes 2 parts the foole and knaue,
    F. B. There is my Recantation in the last Leafe
Writt like a Ciceronian in pure lattin,
    Wh. B. Pure honestie, the playner lattin serues then,
105   *Bl. Kt.* Plague of those pestilent pamphletts, those are they
That wound our cause to the heart,
    Bl. B. Here comes more Anger,
    Bl. Kt. But wee come well prouided for this Storme,
                                Enter Wh. Qs. pawne
    Wh. Q. Is this my pawne? shee that should guard our person
110 Or some pale Fygure of Deiection
Her shape usurping? sorrowe and affrightment
Has præuaylde strangelie wth her;
    Wh. Qs. p. King of Integritie!
Queene of the same, and all the house professors
115 Of noble Candor, uncorrupted Justice
And truth of heart, through my alone discouerie
My life and honor wondrouslie preserude
I bring into youre Knowledge wth my sufferings
Fearefull affrightments, and heart-killing Terrors,
120 The great Incendiarie of Christendome,
The absolutst Abuser of true Sanctitie
Faire peace and holie order, can bee found
In anie part of the Vniuersall Globe
Who making meeke Deuotion keepe the doore

His lips being full of holie Zeale at first,   *125*
Would haue committed a fowle Rape uppon mee,
  Wh. Q. Hah!
  Wh. K. A Rape! that's fowle indeed, the uerie sound
To our Eare fowler then the offence it selfe
To some Kings of the Earth;   *130*
  Wh. Qs. p. Sir, to proceede,
Gladlie I offerd life to preserue honor
Wch would not bee accepted wthout both
The cheife of his ill Ayme being at my honor,
Till heauen was pleasde by some unlookte for accident   *135*
To giue mee courage to redeeme my selfe
  Wh. K. When wee finde desperate Sins in Ill mens
    companies
Wee place a charitable Sorrowe there
But custome and theire leprous Inclination
Quitts us of wonder, for our expectation   *140*
Is answerd in theire liues, but to finde Sin,
I, and a Mrpeice of darknes, shelterd
Under a Robe of Sanctitie, is able
To drawe all wonder to that monster onelie
And leaue created Monsters unadmirde;   *145*
The pride of him that tooke first fall for pride
Is to bee Angell shapte, and imitate
The forme from whence hee fell, but this offender
Far baser then Sins Master, first by Vowe
To holie Order, wch is Angells method   *150*
Takes pride to use that Shape to bee a Deuill;
It greiues mee that my knowledge must be taynted
Wth his infected Name;
Oh rather wth thy finger poynt him out,
  Wh. Qs. p. The place wch hee should fill is uoyde, my L, *155*
His Guilt has ceazde him; the Bl. Bishops pawne;
  Bl. B. Hah! mine? my pawne? the Glorie of his Order;
The prime and præsident Zelot of the Earth,
Impudent pawne! for thy sake at this minute
Modestie suffers, all thats Vertuous blushes,   *160*

And Truths selfe like the Sun uext wth a mist
Lookes red with Anger,
   Wh. B. Bee not you drunck wth rage too,
   Bl. B. Sober Synceritye! nor you a Cup
165 Spicst wth Hypocrisie;
   Wh. Kt. You name there Bishop
But youre owne Christmas Bowle, youre mornings draught
Next youre Episcopall heart all the 12 dayes
Wch Smack you cannot leaue all the yeare following
170   *Bl. Kt.* A shrewde Retort!
H'as made our Bishop smell of burning to,
Would I stood farder off wer't no Impeachment
To my honor or the Game, would they'de playe faster;
White Knight! there is acknowledgd from our house
175 A Reuerence to you, and a Respect
To that lou'de Duke stands next you, wth the fauour
Of the white king, and the forenamde Respected,
I combate wth this cause, if wth all speede
Waste not one Sillable (unfortunate pawne)
180 Of what I speake, thou dost not pleade distraction,
A plea wch will but fayntlie take thee off neyther
From this Leuiathan Scandall, that lyes rowling
Uppon the Crystall waters of Deuotion,
Or what maye quitt thee more, though ynough, nothing,
185 Fall downe and foame, and by that Pang discouer
The uexing Spirit of Falshood strong wthin thee,
Make thy selfe readie for perdition,
There's no Remoue in all the Game to scape it,
This pawne, or this, the Bishop or my selfe
190 Will take thee in the end playe how thou canst;
   Wh. Qs. p. Spite of Sins glorious ostentation,
And all lowde threats those Thundercraks of pride
Ushring a Storme of malice, house of Impudence
Craft and Æquiuocation, my true cause
195 Shall keepe the path it treads in
   Bl. Kt. I playe thus then;
Now in the hearing of this high assemblie

76

Bring forth the Time of this Attempts conception,
    Wh. Qs. p. Conception! oh how tenderlie you handle it,
    Wh. B. It seemes black Knight you are afrayde to touch it, *200*
    Bl. Kt. Well its Eruption, will you haue it so then,
Or you white Bishop for her, the uncleaner
Vile and more Impious, that you Vrge the strayne to,
The greater will her Shames heape showe ith end
And the wrongd meeke mans glorie, the time, pawne!   *205*
    Wh. Qs. p. Yesterdayes cursed Euening,—
    Bl. Kt. Oh the treasure
Of my Reuenge I cannot spend all on thee,
Ruine ynough to spare for all thy Kinred too,
For honors sake call in more Slanderers   *210*
I haue such plentifull confusion,
I knowe not how to waste it, Ile bee nobler yet
And put her to her owne house, King of meekenes
Take the cause to thee, for our hands too heauie,
Our proofes will fall uppon her like a Tower   *215*
And grinde her Bones to powder;
    Wh. Qs. p. What new Engine
Has the Deuill raysde in him now?
    Bl. Kt. Is it hee?
And that the Time, stand firme now to youre Scandall   *220*
Praye do not shift youre Slander,
    Wh. Qs. p. Shift youre Trecheries
They'ue worne one Suite too long,
    Bl. Kt. That holie Man
So wrongfullie accusde by this lost pawne,   *225*
Has not beene seene these 10 dayes in these parts,
    Wh. Kt. How!
    Bl. Kt. Naye at this instant 30 leagues from hence,
    Wh. Qs. p. Fadomlesse Falshood will it scape unblasted!
    Wh. K. Can you make this appeare?   *230*
    Bl. Kt. Light is not cleerer,
By his owne Letters, most Impartiall Monarch!
    Wh. Ks. p. How wrongfullie maye sacred Vertue suffer (Sir)
    Bl. Kt. Bishop wee haue a Treasure of that false heart,

235 *Wh. K.* Step forth and reach those proofes;
     Wh. Qs. p. Amazement couers mee,
     Can I bee so forsaken of a cause
     So strong in truth and æquitie? will uertue
     Send mee no Ayde in this hard time of Frendship?
240 *Bl. Kt.* Theres an Infallible Staff, and a Red Hat
     Reserud for you;
       Wh. Ks. p. Oh Sir endeerde,
       Bl. Kt. A Staff
     That will not easilie breake you maye trust to it,
245 And such a one had youre Corruption neede of
     Theres a State figg for you now,
       Wh. K. Behold all,
     How they cohære in one, I alwayes held
     A charitie so good to holines profest
250 I euer beleiude rather
     The Accuser false then the professor uitious
       Bl. Kt. A charitie like all youre Vertues else
     Gratious and glorious,
       Wh. K. Where settles the offence
255 Let the faults punishment bee deriude from thence
     Wee leaue her to youre censure,
       Bl. Kt. Most iust maiestie;
       Wh. Qs. p. Calamitie of Vertue! my Queene leaue mee too;
     Am I cast off as th'Oliue casts her Flower?
260 Poore Harmlesse Innocence art thou left a Prey
     To the Deuourer?
       Wh. Kt. No thou art not lost
     Let 'em put on theire bloudiest Resolutions
     If the fayre policie I ayme at prospers,
265 Thy Councell Noble Duke!
       Wh. D. For that worke cheerefullie,
       Wh. Kt. A man for speede now!
       Wh. Bs. p. Let it bee my honor, Sir,
     Make mee that Flight that owes her my lifes Seruice,

                                        —exeunt
270 *Bl. Kt.* Was not this brought about well for our honors,

Bl. B. Push, that Galician Skonce can worke out wonders,
Bl. Kt. Letts use her, as uppon the like discouerie
A mayde was usde at Venice, euerie one
Bee readie wth a pennance, begin Maiestie,
Vessell of foolish Scandall! Take thy freight   *275*
Had there beene in that Cabinet of Nicenes
Halfe the Virginities of the earth lockt up
And all swept at one cast by the Dexteritie
Of a Jesuiticall Gamster, 'tad not Valued
The least part of that generall worth thou hast taynted,   *280*
　Bl. K. First I enioyne thee to a 3 dayes fast fort
　Bl. Q. Youre too penurious Sir, Ile make it foure,
　Bl. B. I, to a 12 howers kneeling at one time,
　Bl. Kt. And in a Roome fild all wth Aretines pictures
More then the twice 12 labours of Luxurie,   *285*
Thou shalt not see so much as the chast Pummell
Of Lucrece Dagger peeping, naye, Ile punnish thee
For a Discouerie, Ile torment thy modestie,
　Bl. D. After that 4 dayes Fast to the Inquisition house
Strengthned wth bread and Water for worse pennance,   *290*
　Bl. Kt. Why well sayde Duke of our house noblie
　　aggrauated;
　Wh. Qs. p. Vertue! to showe her Influence more strong,
Fitts me wth patience mightier then my wrong.

ex—t.

INCIPIT ACTUS TERTIUS.   [III, i.]

(· . ·)

Enter Fat Bishop.

F. B. I knowe my pen drawes bloud of the black house,
Theres neuer a Booke I write but theire cause bleedes,
It has lost manye an Ounce of Reputation
Since I came of this side, I strike deepe in
And leaue the Orifex gushing where I come;   *5*
But where's my aduancement all this while I ha' gapte fort,

Ide haue some round preferment corpulent dignitie
That beares some breadth and compasse in the Gift on't,
I am perswaded that this Flesh would fill
10 The biggest Chayre Ecclesiasticall
If it were put to Tryall,
To bee made Master of an Hospitall
Is but a kinde of diseasde Bed-rid honor,
Or Deane of the poore Alms Knights that weare badges,
15 There's but 2 lazye beggarlie preferments
In the White Kingdome, and I haue got 'em both
My Merit do's begin to bee Crop-sick
For want of other Titles   *Enter Bl. Kt.*
    Bl. Kt. Oh here walkes
20 His fulsome holines, now for the Master-Trick
T'undoo him euerlastinglie thats putt home
And make him hang in hell most seriouslie
That iested wth a Halter uppon mee;
    F. B. The black Knight! I must looke to my playe then,
25   *Bl. Kt.* I bring fayre Greetings to youre reuerend Vertues
From Cardinall paulus, youre most princelie kinsman,
    F. B. Our princelie kinsman sayst thou? wee accept 'em,
Praye keepe youre side and distance, I am charie
Of my Episcopall person,
30 I knowe the knights walke in this game too well,
Hee maye skip ouer mee, and where am I then,
    Bl. Kt. There where thou shalt bee shortlie if art fayle not

the Letter

    F. B. Right reuerend and Noble,—meaning our selfe,—
            our true kinsman in bloud, but alienated in affection,
35   youre unkinde Disobedience to the Mother cause,
            prooues at this time the onelie cause of youre ill
            fortune, my present Remoue by Election to the
            Papall dignitie had now auspitiously settled you in
            my Sede Vacante,—hah! had it so?—wch by my next
40   Remoue by Death might haue prooud youre Step to
            Supremacie;—

Title-page of Quarto III from the copy (Mal. 247) in the Bodleian
Library, Oxford.

How! all my bodies bloud mounts to my face
To looke uppon this Letter:
  Bl. Kt. The pill workes wth him,
  F. B. Thinke on't seriouslie, it is not yet too late   *45*
      thorough the submisse acknowledgment of
      youre disobedience to bee louinglie receiude
      into the brotherlie Bosome of the Conclaue:
This was the Chayre of Ease I euer aymde at
Ile make a Bonfire of my Bookes immediatelie,   *50*
All that are left agaynst that side Ile sacrifize
Pack up my plate and Goods and steale awaye
By night at watergate, it is but penning
Another Recantation, and inuenting
2 or 3 bitter Bookes agaynst the white house   *55*
And then I'me in a tother side agen
As firme as ere I was, as fatt and flourishing,
Black Knight! expect a wonder er't bee long;
You shall see mee one of the Black house shortlie,
  Bl. Kt. Youre holines is merrie wth the Messenger,   *60*
Too happie to bee true, you speake what should bee,
If naturall Compunction toucht you truelie,
Oh y'aue drawen bloud, life-bloud, the bloud of honor,
From youre most deere, youre primatiue mothers heart,
Youre sharpe Inuectiues haue been poynts of speares   *65*
In her sweete tender Sides, the unkinde wounds
Wch a Sonne giues, a Sonne of Reuerence spetially
They ranckle ten times more then the Aduersaries,
I tell you (Sir) youre Reuerend Reuolt
Did giue the fearefullst Blowe to adoration   *70*
Oure cause ere felt, it shooke the uerie Statuës
The Vrnes and Ashes of the Saynted Sleepers,
  F. B. Forbeare, or I shall melt in the place I stand
And let forth a Fat Bishop in sad Sirrop,
Suffizes, I am yours when they least dreame on't,   *75*
Ambitious Fodder, power and riches drawes mee,
When I smell honor thats the lock of Haye
That leades mee through the worlds Feild euerie Waye. *exit.*

Bl. Kt. Here's a sweete Paunch to propagate beleife on,
80 Like the Foundation of a chappell layde
Uppon a Quagmire, I maye number him now
Amongst my inferior pollicyes and not shame 'em;
But let mee a litle solace my designes
Wth the remembrance of some braue ones past
85 To cherish the Futuritie of proiect
Whose motion must bee restlesse, till that great worke
Cald the possession of the world be ours;
Was it not I procurde a pretious safeguard
From the White Kingdome to secure our coasts
90 Gaynst the Infidell pyrate, under prætext
Of more necessitous Expedition;
Who made the Jayles flie open (wthout miracle)
And let the locusts out, those dangerous Flies
Whose propertie is to burne Corne wth touching,
95 The Heretique Granaries feele it to this minute,
And now they haue got amongst the Countrie-Crops
They stick so fast to the conuerted Eares
The lowdest Tempest that Authoritie Rowzes
Will hardlie shake 'em off, they haue theire Dens
100 In ladies Couches, there's safe Groues and Fens,
Naye were they followed and found out by th' Scent,
Palme-Oyle will make a Purseuant relent;
Whose policie was't to put a silencst Muzzle,
On all the Barking Tonguemen of the Time,
105 Made pictures, that were dumbe ynough before
Poore Sufferers in that politick Restraynt
My light Spleene skips and shakes my Ribs to thinke on't
Whilst our drifts walkte uncensurde but in thought,
A whistle or a whisper would bee question'd,
110 In the most fortunate Angle of the World,
The Court has held the Cittie by the Hornes
Whilst I haue milkt her, I haue had good soapes too,
From Countrie ladies for theire liberties,
From some, for theire most uaynlie hopde preferments
115 High offices in the Ayre, I should not liue

But for this Mell Aerium, this Mirth-Manna:
My pawne! how now! the Newes!

Enter his pawne

  Bl. Kts. p. Expect none uerie pleasing
That comes (Sir) of my bringing, I'me for sad things,
  Bl. Kt. Thy Conscience is so tender—hoofte alate   *120*
Euerie Nayle pricks it,
  Bl. Kts. p. This maye prick yours too
If there bee anye quick Flesh in a Yard on't,
  Bl. Kt. Mine?
Mischeife must finde a deeper Nayle and a Driuer   *125*
Beyond the strenght of anye Machiauill
The politick kingdomes fatten, to reach mine;
Prethee Compunction! Needle prickt a litle,
Unbinde this sore wound;
  Bl. Kts. p. Sir, youre plotts discouerd;   *130*
  Bl. Kt. Wch of the twentie thousand and nine hundred
Fourescore and fiue, canst tell?
  Bl. Kts. p. Blesse us, so manie?
How doo poore Countrimen haue but one plott
To Keepe a Cowe on, yet in Lawe for that;   *135*
You cannot know 'em all sure by their Names (S^r)
  Bl. Kt. Yes, were theire Number trebled, thou hast seene
A Globe stands on the Table in my Closett?
  Bl. Kts. p. A thing Sir full of Cuntryes, and hard words,
  Bl. Kt. True, wth lines drawen some tropicall, some oblique, *140*
  Bl. Kts. p. I can scarce reade I was brought up in Blindnes;
  Bl. Kt. Just such a thing (if ere my Skull bee opend)
Will my Braynes looke like,
  Bl. Kts. p. Like a Globe of Countries
  Bl. Kt. I, and some Mr-Polititian   *145*
That has sharpe State Eyes will goe neere to pick out
The plotts, and euerie Clymate where they fastend
Twill puzzle 'em too;
  Bl. Kts. p. I'me of youre minde for that Sir,
  Bl. Kt. They'le finde 'em to fall thick uppon some Coūtryes *150*
They'de neede use Spectacles, but I turne to you now,

What plot is that discouerd?
   Bl. Kts. p. Youre last Brat (Sir)
Begot twixt the Black Bishop and youre selfe
155 Youre Antedated letters 'bout the Jesuite,
   Bl. Kt. Discouerd? how?
   Bl. Kts. p. The white Knights policie
Has outstript yours it seemes
Joynd wth the' Assistant Councell of his Duke
160 The Bishops white pawne undertooke the Journey
Who as they saye dischargd it like a Flight
I made him for the Businesse fitt and light
   Bl. Kt. Tis but a bawdie pawne out of the waye a litle,
Enow of them in all parts,
165   *Bl. B.* You haue heard all then?   *Enter Bl. Bishop*
                                    and both the houses
   Bl. Kt. The wonders past wth mee, but some shall downe
     for't,
   Wh. Kt. Set free that Vertuous pawne from all her Wrongs,
Let her bee brought wth honor to the face
Of her malitious Aduersarie,
170   *Bl. Kt.* Good!
   Wh. K. Noble chast Knight, a Title of that Candor
The greatest prince on earth wthout impeachment
Maye haue the dignitie of his worth comprizde in,
This fayre deliuering Act uertue will register
175 In that white Booke of the defence of Virgins
Where the cleere Fame of all preseruing knights
Are to æternal memorie consecrated,
And wee embrace as partner of that honor
This worthie Duke the Councell of the Act
180 Whome wee shall euer place in our Respect,
   Wh. D. Most blest of kings! throand in all royall Graces,
Euerie good Deed sends back its owne reward
Into the bosome of the Enterprizer,
But you to expresse youre selfe as well to bee
185 King of Munificence as Integritie
Adds glorie to the Gift,

   Wh. K. Thy deserts clayme it
Zeale, and Fidelitie, appeare thou bewtie
Of truth and Innocence, best ornament
Of patience, thou that makst thy suffrings glorious,   *190*
   Bl. Kt. Ile take no knowledge on't, what makes shee here?
How dares yond pawne unpennancst, wth a cheeke
Fresh as her Falshood yet, where Castigation
Has left no pale print of her uisiting Anguish
Appeare in this assemblie, lett mee alone   *195*
Sin must bee bold, thats all the Grace tis borne to,
   Wh. Kt. Whats this!
   Wh. K. I'me wonderstruck;
   Wh. Qs. p. Assist mee Goodnes
I shall to prison agen,   *200*
   Bl. Kt. At least I haue mazde 'em,
Scatterd theire Admiration of her Innocence,
As the firde Ships put in seuerd the Fleete
In 88, Ile on wth't, Impudence
Is mischeifes patrimonie, is this Justice?   *205*
Is iniurde Reuerence no sharplier righted,
I euer held that Maiestie impartiall
That like most æquall heauen lookes on the manners
Not on the shapes they shroud in;
   Wh. K. That black Knight   *210*
Will neuer take an answere, tis a Victorie
To make him understand hee dos amisse
When hee knowes in his owne cleere understanding
That hee dos nothing else, showe him the testimonie
Confirmed by goodmen, how that fowle Attempter   *215*
Got but this morning to the place, from whence
Hee dated his forgd lines for ten dayes past:
   Bl. Kt. Why maye not that Corruption sleepe in this
By some Conniuence, as you haue wakte in ours
By too rash Confidence,   *220*
   Wh. D. Ile undertake
That Knight shall teach the deuill how to lye
   Wh. Kt. If Sin were halfe as wise as impudent

Shee'de nere seeke farder for an Aduocate;

Enter Bl. Qs. p.

225   *Bl. Qs. p.* Now to act trecherie wth an Angells Tong
Since alls come out, Ile bring him strangelie in agen;
Where is this iniurde Chastitie, this Goodnes
Whose worth no Transitorie peice can Value
This Rock of constant and inuincible Vertue
230 That made Sins Tempest wearie of his Furie;
     Bl. Q. What is my pawne distracted
     Bl. Kt. I thinke rather
There is some notable Mr-prize of Roguerie
This Drum strikes up for,
235   *Bl. Qs. p.* Let mee fall wth reuerence
Before this blessed Altar,
     Bl. Q. This is madnes
     Bl. Kt. Well, marke the end I stand for Roguerie still
I will not change my Side,
240   *Bl. Qs. p.* I shall bee taxt I knowe,
I care not what the Black house thinkes of mee,
     Bl. Q. What saye you now?
     Bl. Kt. I will not bee unlayde yet;
     Bl. Qs. p. How anie censure flyes, I honor Sanctitie,
245 That is my obiect I entend no other;
I sawe this glorious and most Valiant Vertue
Fight the most noblest Combate wth the Deuill
     Bl. Kt. If both the Bishops had beene there for seconds
Tad beene a compleate Duell;
250   *Wh. K.* Then thou heardst
The Violence entended,
     Bl. Qs. p. Tis a truth
I ioye to iustifie, I was an agent (Sir)
On Vertues part; and raysde that confusde Noyse,
255 That startled his Attempt, and gaue her libertie,
     Wh. Qs. p. Oh tis a righteous Storie shee has told (Sir,)
My life and Fame stand mutuallie engagde,
Both to the truth and Goodnes of this pawne
     Wh. K. Dos it appeare to you yet: cleere as the Sun?

Bl. Kt. Lasse I beleiude it long before twas donne   *260*
Bl. K. Degenerate
Bl. Q. Base
Bl. B. Perfidious
Bl. D. Trayterous Pawne;
Bl. Qs. p. What are you all beside youre selues?   *265*
Bl. Kt. But I.
Remember that pawne!
  Bl. Qs. p. Maye a fearefull Barrennes
Blast both my hopes and pleasures, if I brought not
Her Ruine in my pittie, a new Trap   *270*
For her more sure Confusion,
  Bl. Kt. Haue I wun now?
Did not I saye twas Craft and Machination
I smelt Conspiracie all the waye it went
Although the Messe were couerd, Ime so usde to it,   *275*
  Bl. K. That Queene would I fayne finger,
  Bl. Kt. Youre too hott (Sir)
If shee were tooke, the Game would bee ours quickly,
My Aymes at that white Knight, entrap him first
The Duke will followe too,   *280*
  Bl. B. I would that Bishop
Were in my Diocesse, Ide soone change his whitenes,
  Bl. Kt. Sir I could whip you up a pawne immediatly
I knowe where my Game stands,
  Bl. K. Doo it suddenlye   *285*
Aduantage least must not bee lost in this playe
  Bl. Kt. Pawne, thou art ours,
  Wh. Kt. Hee's taken by default
By willfull Negligence, guard the sacred persons
Looke well to the white Bishop, for that pawne   *290*
Gaue Guard to the Queene and him in the 3ᵈ place,
  Bl. Kt. See what sure piece you lock youre confidence in,
I made this pawne here by Corruption ours,
As soone as honor by Creation yours,
This whitenes uppon him, is but the Leprousie   *295*
Of pure dissimulation, View him now

87

His heart, and his Intents are of our Colour,   *His upper garment*
   Wh. Kt. Most dangerous Hypocrite   *taken off, hee*
   Wh. Q. One made agaynst us,   *appeares Black*
300   *Wh. D.* His Truth of theire Complexion!   *underneath.*
   Wh. K. Has my Goodnes
Clemencie, loue, and fauour gratious raysed thee
From a Condition next to popular labour
Tooke thee from all the dubitable hazards
305 Of Fortune, her most unsecure aduentures
And grafted thee into a Branch of honor
And dost thou fall from the Top-bough by the rottennes,
Of thy alone Corruption, like a Fruite
That's ouer ripend by the beames of Fauour,
310 Let thy owne weight reward thee, I haue forgot thee,
Integritie of life is so deere to mee
Where I finde falshood or a crying Trespasse
Bee it in anye whome our Grace shines most on
Ide teare 'em from my heart,
315   *Wh. B.* Spoke like heauens Substitute;
   Wh. K. You haue him, wee can spare him, & his shame
Will make the rest looke better to theire Game;
   Bl. Kt. The more cunning wee must use then;
   Bl. K. Wee shall match you
320 Playe how you can, perhaps and mate you too;
   F. B. Is there so much amazement spent on him
Thats but half black, there might bee hope of y^t man,
But how will this house wonder if I stand forth
And showe a whole one instantlie discouer
325 One that's all black where there's no hope at all:
   Wh. K. Ile saye thy heart then iustifies thy Bookes
I long for that discouerie,
   F. B. Looke no farder then,
Beare witnesse all the house I am the man
330 And turne my selfe into the Black house freelie;
I am of this Side now;
   Wh. Kt. Monster nere matcht him:
   Bl. K. This is youre noble worke; Knight,

Bl. Kt. Now Ile halter him,

F. B. Next newes you heare expect my bookes agaynst you   *335*
Printed at Dowaye, Bruxells, or Spoletta:

Wh. K. See his goods ceazde on,

F. B. 'Lasse they were all conuayde
Last night by water to a Taylors house
A frend of the black cause,   *340*

Wh. Kt. A præpard Hypocrite,

Wh. D. Præmeditated Turnecoate,

F. B. Yes, rayle on,   *Exeunt.*
Ile reach you in my writings when I'me gon,

Bl. Kt. Flatter him awhile wth honors, till wee put him   *345*
Uppon some dangerous seruice and then burne him,

Bl. K. This came unlookte for,

Bl. D. How wee ioye to see you

F. B. Now Ile discouer all the whitehouse to you,

Bl. D. Indeed! that will both reconcile and rayse you: *350*

Wh. Ks. p. I rest uppon you, Knight, for my Aduancement,

Bl. Kt. Oh for the Staff, the strong Staff that will hold,
And the red Hat fitt for the Guiltie Mazard
Into the emptie Bagg, knowe thy first waye
Pawnes that are lost, are euer out of playe: *355*

Wh. Ks. p. Howes this?

Bl. Kt. No Replications, you knowe mee,
No doubt ere long youle haue more companie
The Bagg is big ynough, twill hold us all   *exeunt*

Wh. Qs. p. I sue to thee, prethee bee one of us,   *360*
Let my loue win thee, thou hast donne truth this daye,
And yesterdaye mỳ honor noble Seruice
The best pawne of our house could not transcend it,

Bl. Qs. p. My pittie flamde wth Zeale, espetiallie
When I forsawe youre Marriage, then it mounted   *365*

Wh. Qs. p. How marriage!

Bl. Qs. p. That contaminating Act
Would haue spoyld all youre Fortunes, a Rape! blesse us all:

Wh. Qs. p. Thou talkst of marriage,

Bl. Qs. p. Yess, yes, you doo marrie,   *370*

I sawe the man;

    Wh. Qs. p. The Man!

    Bl. Qs. p. An Absolute handsome Gentleman, a Compleate
        one,

You'le saye so when you see him, heyre to 3 Red hatts

375 Besides his generall hopes in the black house,

    Wh. Qs. p. Why sure thou'rt much mistaken for this Man;

Why I haue promist single life to all my Affections,

    Bl. Qs. p. Promise you what you will or I or all of us

There's a Fate rules and ouerrules us all mee thinkes,

380   *Wh. Qs. p.* Why how came you to see, or knowe this
        Mysterie!

    Bl. Qs. p. A magicall Glasse I bought of an Ægiptian

Whose Stone retaynes that Speculatiue Vertue

Presented the Man to mee, youre name brings him

As often as I use it, and meethinkes

385 I neuer haue ynough, person and postures

Are all so pleasing,

    Wh. Qs. p. This is wondrous strange

The faculties of soule are still the same,

I can feele no one Motion tend that waye,

390   *Bl. Qs. p.* Wee do not alwayes feele our fayth wee liue by,

Nor euer see our Growth, yet both worke upward,

    Wh. Qs. p. Twas well applied, but maye I see him too,

    Bl. Qs. p. Surelie you maye wthout all doubt or feare

Obseruing the right use as I was taught it,

395 Not looking back, or questioning the Specter,

    Wh. Qs. p. Thats no hard Obseruation, trust it wth mee

Ist possible? I long to see this man,

    Bl. Qs. p. Praye followe mee then and Ile ease you instantlie;

                                  exeunt

           Enter a Bl. Jesting pawne   [III, ii.]

    Bl. Jest. p. I would so fayne take one of these white pawnes
        now,

Ide make him doo all under Drudgerie,

Feede him wth Asses Milke crumbd wth Goates cheese,

And all the whitmeats could bee deuisde for him,
I'de make him my white Jennet when I prauncst   5
After the black knights litter;
   Wh. p. And you would looke then   *Enter a Wh. Pawne*
Just like the Deuill striding o're a Night-Mare
Made of a Millers daughter.
   Bl. p. A pox on you   10
Were you so neere, I'me taken like a Black-bird
In the great Snowe this white pawne grinning ouer mee,
   Wh. p. And now because I will not fowle my Cloaths
Euer hereafter, for white quicklie soyles, you knowe,
   Bl. p. I prethee gett thee gon then I shall smut thee,   15
   Wh. p. Naye Ile put that to Venture now I haue snapt thee,
Thou shalt doo all the durtie-Drudgerie
That Slauerie was e're put to,
   Bl. p. I shall coozen you
You maye chance come and finde youre worke undon then,   20
For I'me too proud to labour, Ile starue first
I tell you that before hand
   Wh. p. I will fitt you then
Wth a black whip that shall not bee behinde hand
   Bl. p. Puh, I haue beene usde to Whipping I haue whipt   25
My selfe 3 mile out of Towne in a morning and
I can fast a fortnight and make all youre meate
Stinck and lye a youre hands!
   Wh. p. To præuent that youre foode shall be Blackberries,
And uppon Gawdie dayes a pickled Spyder   30
Cut out like an Anchouis, I'me not to learne
A Munckeys ordinarie, come sir, will you friske?
                    Enter a 2 Black pawne
   2. Bl. p. Soft, soft you, you haue no such bergayne of it,
If you looke well about you,
   Wh. p. By this hand   35
I am snapt too, a Black Pawne in the Breech of mee,
Wee three looke like a Birdspit, a white Chick
Between 2 Russet woodcocks:—
   1. Bl. p. I'me so glad of this

40   *Wh. p.* But you shall haue small cause, for Ile firke you
    2. Bl. p. Then Ile firke you agen,
    Wh. p. And Ile firke him agen,
    Bl. p. Masse, here will bee ould firking; I shall haue
the worst ont I can firke no bodie, wee drawe
45 together now for all the world like 3 Flyes wth
one Strawe thorough theire Buttocks   *exeunt*

      Enter Bl. Qs. p. and Wh. Qs. p.   [III, iii.]

    Bl. Qs. p. This is the Roome hee did appeare to mee in,
And looke you this the Magicall glasse that show'de him,
    Wh. Qs. p. I finde no Motion yet, what should I thinke on't,
A Suddayne feare inuades mee, a faynt trembling
5 Under this omen
As is oft felt the panting of a Turtle
Under a Stroaking hand
    Bl. Qs. p. That boades good luck still,
Signe you shall change state speedilie, for that trembling
10 Is alwayes the first Symptome of a Bride
For anie Vayner feares that maye accompanie
His Apparition, by my truth to Frendship
I quit you of the least, neuer was obiect
More gracefullie presented, the uerie Ayre
15 Conspires to doo him honor, and creates
Sweete Vocall Sounds as if a Bridegroome enterd
Wch argues the blest Harmonie of youre loues:
    Wh. Qs. p. And will the using of my name produce him?
    Bl. Qs. p. Naye of youres onelie else the Wonder halted,
20 To cleere you of that doubt Ile put the difference
In practise, the first thing I doo, and make
His Inuocation in the names of others
    Wh. Qs. p. Twill satisfye mee much that
    Bl. Qs. p. It shall bee donne

        the Inuocation

25   Thou whose gentle Forme and face
    Fild latelie this Ægiptick glasse

By the Imperious-powerfull name
And the Vniuersall Fame
Of the mightie black-house Queene
I coniure thee to bee seene: *30*
What! see you nothing yet?
  Wh. Qs. p. Not anie part;
Pray, trie another
  Bl. Qs. p. You shall haue youre will
I double my command and power   *35*
And at the Instant of this hower
Inuoke thee in the white Queenes Name,
Wth staye for Time, and Shape the same;
What see you yet?
  Wh. Qs. p. There's nothing showes at all   *40*
  Bl. Qs. p. My Truth reflects the cleerer, then now fixe
And blesse youre fayre Eyes wth youre owne for euer,
  Thou well composde by Fates hand drawen
  To enioye the white Queenes pawne,
  Of whome Thou shalt (by Vertue met)   *45*
  Manye gracefull Issues gett,
  By the bewtie of her Fame
  By the whitenes of her Name,
  By her fayre and fruitfull loue
  By her Truth that mates the Doue   *50*
  By the Meeknes of her Minde
  By the softnes of her kinde
  By the Lustrë of her Grace
  By all these thou art summond to this place,
Harke, how the Ayre enchanted wth youre prayses   *55*
And his approach those words to sweete Notes rayses:

               Musique, enter the Jesuite in
               rich attire like an Apparition
               presents himselfe before
               the Glasse, then exit.

Wh. Qs. p. Oh lett him staye awhile, a litle longer,
Bl. Qs. p. Thats a good hearing;
Wh. Qs. p. If hee bee mine why should hee part so soone?

93

60 *Bl. Qs. p.* Why this is but the Shadowe of yours; how do you?
   Wh. Qs. p. Oh I did ill to giue consent to see it;
   What Certayntie is in our bloud or State
   What wee still write is blotted out by Fate,
   Our Wills are like a cause that is Lawe-tost,
65 What one Court orders is by another crost
   Bl. Qs. p. I finde no fitt place for this passion here,
   Tis meerelie an Intruder, hee is a Gentleman
   Most wishfullie composde honor growes on him
   And wealth pilde up for him, h'as youth ynough too
70 And yet in the Sobrietie of his Countenance
   Graue as a Tetrarch, wch is gratious
   In the eye of modest pleasure, where's the emptines?
   What can you more request?
   Wh. Qs. p. I do not knowe
75 What answere yet to make! it do's require
   A Meeting twixt my feare and my desire,
   Bl. Qs. p. Shees caught, and wch is strange by her most
            wronger   *exeunt*
                  Finit Actus 3ᵘˢ

            INCIPIT QUARTUS.   [IV, i.]

         Enter Bl. Kts. pawne meeting the black Bˢ pawne
                  richlie accoultred.

   Bl. Kts. p. Tis hee, my Confessor! hee might ha' past mee
   7 yeare together, had I not by chance
   Aduanced mine Eye uppon that letterd hattband
   The Jesuiticall Symbole to bee knowne by,
    5 Worne by the braue Colledgians by Consent;
   Tis a strange habit for a holie Father
   A president of pouertie espetiallie,
   But wee the Sonnes and daughters of Obedience
   Dare not once thinke awrie, but must confesse ourselues
10 As humblie to the Father of that Fether

                        94

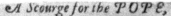

A Scourge for the POPE,

Satyrically scourging the itching sides of his obstinate
Brood, in ENGLAND.

To the tune of *Roome for &c.*

A disguized Iesuite.

FAmous Brittany,
Giue thankes to God on high,
Who hath deliuered thee

Long haue they looked
To get toleration,
But God kept the heart

Now we shall haue
No secret Assemblies,
Nor meeting houses

A disguised Jesuit. From a broadside in the Pepys Library,
Magdalene College, Cambridge.

Long Spur and poniard, as to the Albe and Altar,
And happie wee'are so highlye gracde to attayne to it,
Holie and Reuerend!

   Bl. Bs. p. How hast found mee out?

   Bl. Kts. p. Oh Sir, put on the Sparklingst Trim of glorie   *15*
Perfection will shine formost, and I knowe you
By the Catholicall Marke you weare about you,
The marke aboue youre forehead;

   Bl. Bs. p. Are you growen
So ambitious in youre obseruance? well, youre busines?   *20*
I haue my Game to followe,

   Bl. Kts. p. I haue a worme
Followes mee so that I can followe no Game,
The most faynt-hearted pawne if hee could see his playe,
Might snap mee up at pleasure, I desire (Sir)   *25*
To bee absolute, my Conscience being at ease
I could then wth more courage plie my Game:

   Bl. Bs. p. Twas a base Fact

   Bl. Kts. p. Twas to a Schismatick pawne (Sir)

   Bl. Bs. p. Whats that to the Nobilitie of Reuenge   *30*
Suffizes, I haue neyther will nor power
To giue you absolution for that Violence
Make youre Petition to the Pennance-Chamber,
If the Taxe-Register releiue you in't
By the black Bishops clemencie, you haue wrought out   *35*
A singular peice of fauour wth youre monie,
Thats all youre refuge now;

   Bl. Kts. p. This sting shootes deeper   *exit.*

   Bl. Bs. p. Yonders my Game, wch like a politique Chesse Mr:
I must not seeme to see;   { *Enter wh. Qs. p. and* *40*

   Wh. Qs. p. Oh my heart!   {   *Bl. Qs. p.*

   Bl. Qs. p. That tis!

   Wh. Qs. p. The uerie selfe same, that the magicall Mirror
Presented latelie to mee,

   Bl. Qs. p. And how like   *45*
A most regardlesse Stranger hee walkes by
Meerelie ignorant of his Fate, you are not minded

The principallst part of him, what strange Mysteries
Inscrutable loue workes by!
50   *Wh. Qs. p.* The time you see
Is not yet come!
      Bl. Qs. p. But tis in our power now
To bring time neerer, Knowledge is a Mastrie,
And make it obserue us, and not wee it:
55   *Wh. Qs. p.* I would force nothing from its proper Vertue,
Let time haue his full course, Ide rather die
The modest death of undiscouerd loue
Then haue heauens least and lowest Seruant suffer
Or in his motion receiue Check for mee;
60 How is my Soules Growth alterd, that single Life
The fittest garment that peace euer made for't,
Is growen too streight, too stubborne on the suddayne;
      Bl. Qs. p. Hee comes this waye agen
      Wh. Qs. p. Oh theres a Traytor
65 Leapt from my heart into my cheeke alreadie
That will betraye all to his powerfull eye
If it but glance uppon mee,
      Bl. Qs. p. By my Veritie,
Looke, hees past by agen, drownd in Neglect
70 Wthout the prosperous hint of so much happines
To looke uppon his fortunes, how closse Fate
Seales up the Eye of humayne Vnderstanding,
Till like the Suns Flower Time and loue uncloses it,
Twere pittie hee should dwell in ignorance longer
75   *Wh. Qs. p.* What will you doo?
      Bl. Qs. p. Yes, dye a bashfull Death, doo,
And let the remedie passe by unusde still
You are changd ynough alreadie, and you'de looke into it,
Absolute Sir, wth youre most noble pardon
80 For this my rude Intrusion, I am bold
To bring the knowledge of a Secret neerer
By manie dayes (Sir) then it would arriue
In its owne proper reuelation wth you,
Praye turne, and fixe, do you knowe yond Noble goodnes

96

Bl. Bs. p. Tis the first minute my Eye blest mee wth her,   *85*
And cleerelie showes how much my knowledge wanted
Not knowing her till now;
    Bl. Qs. p. Shee's to bee likte then,
Praye uiew aduisedlie, there is strong reason
That I'me so bold to urge it, you must ghesse,   *90*
The worke concernes you neerer then you thinke for,
    Bl. Bs. p. Her glorie, and the Wonder of this Secret
Putts a Reciprocall amazement on mee,
    Bl. Qs. p. And tis not wthout worth, you 2 must bee
Better acquaynted;   *95*
    Bl. Bs. p. Is there cause? Affinitie?
Or anie Curteous helpe Creation ioyes in
To bring that forward,
    Bl. Qs. p. Yes, yes, I can showe you
The neerest waye to that perfection   *100*
(Of a most uertuous one) that Joye e're found,
Praye marke her once agen, then.followe mee
And I will showe you her must bee youre wife (Sr)
    Bl. Bs. p. The Mysterie extends, or else Creation
Has sett that admirable peice before us   *105*
To chuse our chast delights by
    Bl. Qs. p. Please you followe, Sir,
    Bl. Bs. p. What Art haue you to putt mee on an Obiect
And cannot gett mee off, tis payne to part from it;   *exit*
    Wh. Qs. p. If there prooue no Check in that Magicall glasse, *110*
But my proportion come as fayre and full
Into his Eye, as his into mine latelie,
Then I'me confirmde hee is mine owne for euer,   *Enter agayn.*
    Bl. Bs. p. The uerye selfe same that the Mirror blest mee wth,
From head to foote, the bewtie and the Habit;   *115*
Kept you this place still? did you not remoue, ladie?
    Wh. Qs. p. Not a foote farder (Sir)
    Bl. Bs. p. Ist possible,
I would haue sworne I'de seene the substance yonder,
Twas to that lustrë, to that life presented   *120*
    Wh. Qs. p. E'en so was yours to mee (Sir)

Bl. Bs. p. Sawe you mine?

Wh. Qs. p. Perfectlie cleere, no sooner my Name usde

But yours appearde

125 *Bl. Bs. p.* Just so did yours at mine now;

Bl. Qs. p. Why stand you idle, will you let time coosen you

Protracting Time, of those delitious benefitts

That Fate hath markte to you, you modest payre

Of blushing Gamsters and you (Sir) the bashfulst,

130 I can not flatter a fowle fault in anie,

Can you bee more then man and wife assignde,

And by a power the most irreuocable?

Others that bee aduenturers in delight

Maye meete wth Crosses, Shame, or Seperation

135 Theire Fortunes hid, and the Euents lockt from 'em,

You knowe the minde of Fate you must bee coupled:

Bl. Bs. p. Shee speakes but Truth in this, I see no reason then,

That wee should misse the rellish of this night

But that wee are both shamefacst

140 *Wh. Qs. p.* How? this night, Sir,

Did not I knowe you must bee mine, and therein

Youre priuiledge runs strong, for that loose Motion

You neuer should bee; is it not my fortune

To match wth a pure mind, then am I miserable,

145 The Doues and all chast louing winged Creatures

Haue theire payres fitt, theire desires iustlie mated;

Is Woman more Vnfortunate? a Virgin

The Maye of Woman! Fate that has ordaynde (Sir)

Wee should bee man and wife, has not giuen warrant

150 For anie Act of knowledge till wee are so,

Bl. Bs. p. Tender-eyde Modestie, how it giues at this

I'me as far off for all this strange Imposture

As at first Enteruiew, where lyes our Game now?

You knowe I cannot marrie by my Order:

155 *Bl. Qs. p.* I knowe you cannot, Sir, yet you may Venture

Uppon a Contract,

Bl. Bs. p. Hah:

Bl. Qs. p. Surelie you maye Sir,

Wthout all question so far, wthout danger
Or anie Stayne to youre Vowe, and that maye take her,   *160*
Naye doo'te wth speede sheele thinke you mean the better too;
   Bl. Bs. p. Bee not so lauish of that blessed Spring,
Y'aue wasted that uppon a cold occasion now
Would wash a sinfull soule white, by our loue-Joyes
That motion shall ne're light uppon my Tong more   *165*
Till weere contracted, then I hope y'are mine
   Wh. Qs. p. In all iust dutie euer,
   Bl. Qs. p. Then, do you question it?
Push, then y'are man and wife all but Church Ceremony,
Praye letts see that donne first, shee shall doo reason then,   *170*
Now Ile enioye the Sport and coozen you both,
My blouds game is the Wages I haue workte for   *ex—t.*

Enter Bl. Kt. wth his pawne   [IV, ii.]

   Bl. Kt. Pawne I haue spoke to the fat Bishop for thee,
I'le gett thee Absolution from his owne mouth;
Reach mee my chayre of ease, my chayre of coosnage
7 thousand pound in weomen reach mee that
I loue a life to sitt uppon a Banck   *5*
Of heretique Gold, oh soft and gentlie, sirrah,
Theres a fowle Flawe in the Bottome of my Drum; p.
I ne're shall make sound Souldier, but sound Trecher
Wth anie hee in Europe, how now, Qualme!
Thou hast the pukingst Soule that ere I met wth   *10*
It cannot beare one Suckling Villanie,
Mine can digest a Monster wthout cruditie
A Sin as Weightie as an Elephant
And neuer wamble for't;
   Bl. Kts. p. I, you haue beene usde to it, Sir,   *15*
Thats a great helpe, the swallowe of my Conscience
T'as but a narrowe passage you must thinke yet
It lyes in the pœnitent pipe and will not downe
If I had got 7 thousand pound by offices
And guld downe that, the Boare would haue bin bigger;   *20*
   Bl. Kt. Naye, if thou prooust facetious I shall hugg thee

99   7-2

Can a soft, Reare, poore-pocht Iniquitie
So ride uppon thy Conscience I'me ashamde of thee,
Hadst thou betrayde the whitehouse to the black
25 Beggard a Kingdome by dissimulation
Vnioynted the fayre frame of peace and Traffique,
Poysond Alleagance, sett fayth back, and wrought
Weomens soft soules e'en up to masculine Malice
To persue truth to death if the cause rowzd 'em,
30 That Stares and Parrotts are first taught to curse thee
    Bl. Kts. p. I marrie Sir, heres swapping Sins indeed,
    Bl. Kt. All these and ten times trebled, has this Brayne
Beene parent to, they are my offsprings all,
    Bl. Kts. p. A goodlie broode!
35   *Bl. Kt.* Yet I can iest as titelie
Laugh and tell stirring Stories to Court Maddames
(Daughters of my Seducement) wth alacritie
As high and heartie, as youths time of Innocence
That neuer knewe a Sin to shape a sorrowe by
40 I feele no tempest not a Leafe wind stirring
To shake a fault my Conscience is becalmd rather,
    Bl. Kts. p. Ime sure there is a whirlewinde huffs in mine Sir,
    Bl. Kt. Sirrah, I haue sold the Groome a'th Stoole 6 times,
And receiude monye of 6 seuerall Ladies
45 Ambitious to take place of Barronets Wiues,
To 3 ould Mummie-Matrons, I haue promist
The Mothership a'th Maydes, I haue taught o^r frends too
To conuey white house Gold to our black Kingdome
In cold bakte pasties and so coozen Searchers,
50 For Venting hallowed Oyle, Beads, Meddalls, pardons,
Pictures, Veronicaes heads in priuate presses,
Thats don by one ith habit of a Pedler
Letters conuayd in Roules, Tobacco-Balls
When a Restraynt comes by my politique Councell
55 Some of our Jesuites turne Gentlemen Vshers,
Some Faulkners, some park keepers, & some Huntsmen,
One tooke the Shape of an ould Ladies Cooke once
And dispacht 2 Chares in a Sundaye morning

The Altar and the Dresser! praye what use
Put I my Summer Recreation to?   *60*
But more to informe my knowledge in the State
And strenght of the White Kingdome! no fortificatiõ
Hauen, Creeke, Landing place 'bout the white Coast
But I got draught and platforme, learnd the depth
Of all theire channells, knowledge of all Sands   *65*
Shelues, rocks, and riuers for inuasion proper'st
A Catalogue of all the Nauie Royall
The Burden of the Ships, the Brassie Murderers,
The number of the men, to what Cape bound;
Agen, for the discouerie of the Inlands,   *70*
Neuer a Sheire but the State better knowen
To mee then to the Brest Inhabitants
What power of men and horse, Gentries Reuennues,
Who well affected to our Side, who ill
Who neyther well nor ill, all the Neutrallitie,   *75*
Thirtie eight thousand Soules haue been seducd, P.
Since the Jayles Vomited wth the pill I gaue 'em.

   Bl. Kts. p. Sure you put Oyle of toade into that phisick (Sr).
   Bl. Kt. I'me now about a Mr: peice of playe
To entrap the white Knight and wth false allurements   *80*
Entice him to the black house, more will followe
Whil'st our Fat Bishop setts uppon the Queene
Then will our Game lye sweetelye;
   Bl. Kts. p. Hee's come now Sir,   *Enter Fat Bishop,*
   F. B. Here's Taxa pœnitentiaria, knight;   *85*
The Booke of generall pardons of all prices
I haue beene searching for his Sin this halfe hower,
And cannot light uppon't,
   Bl. Kt. That's strange, let mee see it,
   Bl. Kts. p. Pawne wretched that I am, has my rage don that *90*
There is no præsident of pardon for,
   Bl. Kt. For wilfull murder, thirteene pound foure
shillings and sixepence—thats reasonable cheape, for
killing, killing, killing, killing, killing, killing,
Why here's nothing but killing Bishop of this side,   *95*

    F. B. Turne the Sheete ouer, you shall finde Adulterie
And other triuiall Sins,
    Bl. Kt. Adulterie? oh I'me in't now,
For Adulterie a Couple of Shillings, and for fornication five
        pence
100 Masse, those are 2 good penniworths, I cannot see
how a man can mend himselfe,—for Lieing wth
mother, Sister, and daughter—I marrie Sir, thirtie
three pound 3 shilling, 3 pence,—
The Sins gradation right payde all in threes too,
105   *F. B.* You haue read the Storie of that Monster (Sir)
That got his daughter, Sister and his wife
Of his owne Mother—
    Bl. Kt. Simonie, nine pound
    F. B. They maye thanke mee for that, twas nineteene
110 Before I came,
I have mitigated manye of the Soms,
    Bl. Kt. Sodomie sixpence, you should put that Summe euer
On the Backside of youre Booke, Bishop;
    F. B. There's fewe on's uerie forward (Sir,)
115   *Bl. Kt.* Whats here (Sir) 2 ould præsidents of
        Encouragement,
    F. B. I those are Antient Notes
    Bl. Kt. Giuen as a Gratuitie for the killing of an
hæreticall prince wth a poysond knife ducketts 5
thousand
120   *F. B.* True Sir, that was payde
    Bl. Kt. Promised also to Doctor Lopez for poyson-
ning the Mayden Queene of the white kingdome
ducketts 20 thousand, wch sayde Summe was afterwards giuen as a meritorious Almes to the Nun-
125 nerie at Lisbon, hauing at this present ten
thousand pound more at vse in the Townehouse
of Antwerpe!
    Bl. Kts. p. Whats all this to my Conscience (worthie Holines)
I sue for pardon, I haue brought monye wth mee
130   *F. B.* You must depart, you see there is no præsident

Of anie price or pardon for youre fact,
 Bl. Kts. p. Most miserable, are fowler sins remitted?
Killing, naye willfull murder,
 F. B. True, there's instance,
Were you to kill him I would pardon you   *135*
There's president for that and price sett downe,
But none for Gelding;
 Bl. Kts. p. I haue pickt out Vnderstanding now for euer
Out of that Cabalistique bloudie Riddle
Ile make awaye all my estate and Kill him   *140*
And by that act obtaine full absolution.   *exit.*
            Enter Bl. King.
 Bl. K. Why Bishop! Knight! wheres youre Remoues? youre
  Traps?
Stand you now idle in the heate of Game?
 Bl. Kt. My life for yours, black Soueraigne, the Games ours
I haue wrought under hand for the white Knight   *145*
And his braue Duke and find 'em coming both
 F. B. Then for theire sanctimonious Queenes surprizall
In this State puzzle and distracted hurrie
Trust my Arch subteltie wth,
 Bl. K. Oh Eagle-pride   *150*
Neuer was Game more hopefull of our Side:
 Bl. Kt. If Bishop Bulbeefe bee not snapt next Boute
As the Men stand Ile neuer trust Art more:

              exeunt

      Enter Bl. Queenes pawne as   [IV, iii.]
       conducting the White to a
       chamber, then fetching in
       the Bl. Bishops pawne the
       Jesuite conuayes him to
       another puts out the light
       and shee followes.

    Enter White Knight, and wh. Duke.   [IV, iv.]
 Wh. Kt. True Noble Duke, fayre Vertues most endeerd one
Let us præuent theire ranck Insinuation

Wth Truth of cause and courage, meete theire Plots
Wth confident goodnes that shall strike 'em groueling
5 *Wh. D.* Sir all the Jins, Traps and alluring snares
The Deuill has beene at worke since 88 on
Are layde for the Great Hope of this Game onlie,
Wh. Kt. Why the more Noble will truths Triumph bee,
When they haue woond about our constant Courages
10 The glitteringst Serpent that ere falshood fashiond
And glorieing most in theire resplendent poysons
Just Heauen can finde a Bolt to bruize his head;
Wh. D. Looke, would you see distruction lye a sunning
In yonder smile sitts bloud and Trecherie basking *Enter*
15 In that perfidious Modell of Face-Falshood *Bl. Knight*
Hell is drawen grinning,
Wh. Kt. What a payne it is
For Truth to fayne a litle,
Bl. Kt. Oh fayre knight!
20 The rising Glorie of that house of Candor,
Haue I so manie protestations lost,
Lost, lost, quite lost, am I not worth youre confidence?
I that have uowde the Faculties of soule
Life spirit, and Brayne to youre sweete Game of youth
25 Youre noble fruitfull Game, can you mistrust
Anie fowle playe in mee, that haue beene euer
The most submisse Obseruer of youre Vertues
And no waye taynted wth Ambition
Saue onelie to bee thought youre first Admirer,
30 How often haue I changd for youre delight
The royall præsentation of my place
Into a Mimick Jester, and become
Of a graue State-Sire a light Sonne of pastime
Made three score yeares a Tomboye, a meere Wanton
35 Ile tell you what I told a Sauoye Dame once,
New wed, high, plumpe and lusting for an Issue,
Wthin the yeare I promisd her a childe
If shee could stride ouer St Rumbants breeches
A Rellique kept at Mechlin, the next morning

One of my followers ould hose was conuayde   *40*
Into her chamber where shee tryde the Feate,
By that and a Court Frend after grewe great
  Wh. Kt. Why who could bee wthout thee
  Bl. Kt. I will change
To anye shape to please you, and my Ayme   *45*
Has beene to win youre loue in all this Game
  Wh. Kt. Thou hast it Noblie, and wee long to see
The Black house pleasure State and dignitie
  Bl. Kt. Of honor you'le so surfett and delight
Youle nere desire agen to see the white: *50*
                                    exeunt
                          Enter Wh: Queene
  Wh. Q, My loue, my hope, my deerest, oh hees gon,
Ensnarde, entrapt, surprizde amongst the Black-ons
I neuer felt Exstremitie like this
Thick Darknes Dwells uppon this hower, Integritie
(Like one of heauens bright luminaries now   *55*
By Errors dullest Element interposde)
Suffers a black Eclips—I neuer was
More sick of loue, then now I am of horror   *Enter Fat*
I shall bee taken, the Games lost, Ime sett uppon   *Bp.*
Oh tis the Turne-coate Bishop, hauing wachd   *60*
The Aduantage of his plaie, Comes now to ceaze on mee
Oh Ime hard besette Distressd most miserablye
  F. B. Tis uaine to stir, remoue wch way you can
I take you now, this is the time wee euer hopde for,
Queene you must downe;   *65*
  Wh. Q, No rescue no Deliuerance
  F. B. The Black Kings bloud burnes for thy Prostitution
And nothing but the Spring of thy chast vertu
Can coole his Inflamation, instantly
Hee dyes uppon a plurisie of Luxurie   *70*
If hee deflowre thee not,   *Enter Wh: Bishop*
  Wh. Q. Oh straight of miserie;
  Wh. B. And is youre holines his diuine procurer
  F. B. The Diuills int, Ime taken by a Ring-doue

75 Where stoode this Bishop that I sawe him not
    Wh. B. You were so ambitious you lookt ouer mee
    You aimde at no lesse person then the Queene
    The glorie of the game if shee were wun
    The way were open to the Master check
80 Wch,—looke you, hee or his liues to giue you;
    Honor and vertu guide him in his Station
    Wh. Q. Oh: my safe Sanctuarie
    Wh. K. Lett heauens blessings
    Bee mine no longer then I am thy sure one,
85 The doues house is not safer in the Rock
    Then thou in my firme bosome;
    Wh. Q. I am blest int,
    Wh. K. Is it that lumpe of ranck Ingratitude
    Sweld wth the poyson of hipocrisie
90 Could hee bee so malitious, has pertaken
    Of the sweet fertill blessings of our kingdome;
    Bishop; thou hast don our white house gratious Seruice
    And worthy the faire Reuerence of thy place
    For thee (black holines) that workst out thy death
95 As the blinde Mole, the properst Son of earth
    Who in the casting his Ambitious hills up
    Is often taken, and destroide ith midst
    Of his aduanced worke, twere well wth thee
    If like that verminous Labourer, wch thou Imitatst
100 In hills of pride and malice, when death puts thee up
    The silent Graue might prooue thy Bagge for euer
    No deeper pitt then that, for thy uaine hope
    Of the white Knight, and his most firme assistant
    Two Princelye Peices wch I knowe thy Thoughts
105 Giue lost for euer now, my strong Assurance
    Of theire fixt vertues, could you lett in Seas
    Of populous vntruths against that fort
    Twould burst the proudest Billowes,
    Wh. Q. My feares past then,
110   *Wh. K.* Feare? you were neuer guiltie of an Iniurie
    To goodnes, but in that

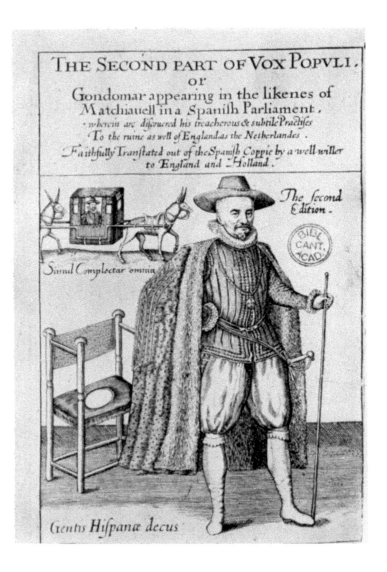

THE SECOND PART OF VOX POPVLI,
or
Gondomar appearing in the likenes of
Matchiauell in a Spanish Parliament,
wherein are discouered his treacherous & subtile Practises
To the ruine as well of England.as the Netherlandes.
Faithfully Tranflated out of the Spanish Coppie by a well-willer
to England and Holland.

The ſecond
Edition.

Simul Complectar omnia

Gentis Hifpanæ decus

Title-page of *The Second Part of Vox Populi* (1624), by Thomas Scott,
showing Gondomar's litter and "chair of ease."

Wh. Q. It staide not wth mee, Sir,

Wh. K. It was too much if it usurpd a thought
Place a good Guard theire

Wh. Q. Confidence is sett, sir,   *115*

Wh. K. Take that prize hence you Reuerend of men
Put couetousnes, into the Bagg agen,

F. B. The bagge had neede be sound, or it goes to wrack
Sine and my weight will make a strong on crack.

Finit Actus Quartus.

INCIPIT QUINTUS.

Musique, Enter the Black Knight   [v, i.]
in his Litter! calls

Bl. Kt. Hold, hold
Is the black Bishops pawne the Jesuite
Planted aboue for his concise Oration?

Bl. Bs. p. Ecce triumphanti me fixum Cæsaris Arce

Bl. Kt. Art there my holie Boye, sirrah, Bishop Tumbrell   *5*
Is snapt, in the Bagg by this time

Bl. Bs. p. Hæretici pereant sic;

Bl. Kt. All lattin! sure the Oration has infected him
Awaye, make haste, theire coming

Hoboyes, Enter Bl. K.
Q. D. meeting the
wh Knight and Duke

the Oration

Si quid mortalibus unquam Oculis hilarem et gra-   *10*
tum aperuit diem, si quid peramantibus amicorum
animis gaudium attulit, peperituè lætitiam (Eques
Candidissime prælucentissime) fælicem profecto tuũ
a domo Candoris ad domum Nigritudinis acces-
sum promisisse, peperisse, attulisse fatemur,   *15*
Omnes aduentus tui conflagrantissimi, Omni qua
possumus lætitia, gaudio, congratulatione, Acclama-

107

tione, Animis Obseruantissimis, Affectibus diuotissimis, obsequiis Venerabundis te sospitem congra-
20   tulamur

    Bl. K. Sir in this short Congratulatorie Speech
You maye conceiue how the whole house affects you,
    Bl. Kt. The Colledges and sanctimonious Seedeplotts,
    Wh. Kt. Tis cleere, and so acknowledgd, (Royall sir)
25   *Bl. Kt.* What honors, pleasures, Rarities, delights
Youre noble thought can thinck
    Bl. Q. Youre faire eye fix on;
Thats comprehended in the spatious circle
Of our black-kingdome, they are youre seruants all
30 *Wh. Kt.* How amplie you endeere vs
    Wh. D. They are fauours
That æquallye enrich the royall giuer
As the receiuer in the free donation
    Bl. Kt. Harke to enlarge youre welcome, from all parts
35 Is heard sweete sounding Ayres, abstruse things open,
Of Voluntarie Freenes, and yond Altar
The Seate of Adoration, seemes to adore
The Vertues you bring wth you,
    Wh. Kt. There's a taste
40 Of the ould Vessell still, the erroneous rellish

                       Musique an Altar discouerd
                            and Statues, wth a Song

Song.

    Wonder worke some strange delight
    This place was neuer yet wthout
    To welcome the fayre Whitehouse Knight,
    And to bring our hopes about
45   Maye from the Altar flames aspire
    Those Tapors set themselues afire
    Maye sencelesse things our Joyes approoue
    And those Brazen Statues moue   *The Images*
    Quickned by some power aboue   *mooue in a*
50   Or what more strange to showe our loue: *dance.*

Bl. Kt. A happie omen waites uppon this hower
All moue portentouslie, the right hand waye,
   Bl. K. Come letts set free all the most choise delights
That euer adorned dayes or quickned Nights.

                               exeunt

           Enter Wh. Qs. p.   [v, ii.]

   Wh. Qs. p. I see twas but a Tryall of my loue now,
H'as a more modest minde, and in that Vertue
Most worthilie has Fate prouided for mee;

                          Enter Jesuite

Hah! tis the bad man in the reuerend habit
Dares hee bee seene agen, traytor to Holinesse,   *5*
Oh Marble Fronted Impudence, and knowes
How much hee has wrongd mee, I'me ashamde hee blushes not,
   Bl. Bs. p. Are you yet storde wth anye womans pittie
Are you the Mistris of so much deuotion
Kindnes and charitie as to bestowe   *10*
An Almes of Loue on youre poore sufferer yet
For youre sake onelie;
   Wh. Qs. p. Sir, for the Reuerence and Respect you ought
To giue to Sanctitie though none to mee,
In being her Seruant uowde and weare the liuerie   *15*
If I might councell you, you should nere speake
The language of Vnchastnes in that habit,
You would not thinke how ill it do's wth you,
The World's a Stage on wch all parts are playde
You'de thinke it most absurd to haue a deuill   *20*
Presented there not in a Deuills shape,
Or wanting one to send him out in yours,
You'de rayle at that for an Absurditie
No Colledge e're committed, for decorums sake then,
For pitties cause, for Sacred Vertues honor,   *25*
If you'le persist still in youre Deuills part
Present him as you should doo, and let one
That carries up the goodnes of the playe
Come in that habit, and Ile speake wth him,

30 Then will the parts bee fitted and the Spectators
Know wch is wch, it must bee strange cunning
To finde it else, for such a one as you
Is able to deceiue a mightie Audience,
Naye, those you haue seducst if there bee anie
35 In the Assemblie, if they see what manner
You playe youre Game wth mee, they cannot loue you,
Is there so little hope of you to smile, Sir?
 Bl. Bs. p. Yes, at youre feares, at the Ignorance of youre
  power,
The litle use you make of Time, youth, Fortune,
40 Knowing you haue a housband for lusts Shelter,
You dare not yet make bold wth a Frends comfort,
This is the plague of Weaknes,
 Wh. Qs. p. So hot-burning
The Sillables of Sin flie from his lips,
45 As if the letter came new cast from hell
 Bl. Bs. p. Well, setting aside the Dish you loathe so much
Wch has beene heartilie tasted by youre Betters,
I come to marrie you to the Gentleman
That last enioyde you, 'hope that pleases you,
50 There's no immodest rellish in that office!
 Wh. Qs. p. Strange of all others hee should light on him,
To tye that holie knott that sought to undoo mee,
Were you requested to performe that office?
 Bl. Bs. p. I name you a sure Token
55 *Wh. Qs. p.* As for that Sir—
Now y'are most welcome, and my fayre hopes of you,
You'le neuer breake the Sacred knott you tye once,
Wth anye lewde Sollicitings hereafter,
 Bl. Bs. p. But all the Craft's in getting of it knit,
60 You're all a fire to make youre coosning market,
I am the marrier, and the man, do you knowe mee?
Do you knowe mee Nice Iniquitie, strickt Luxurie,
And holie whoredome that would clap on Marriage
Wth all hott Speede to soader up youre Game,
65 See what a Scourge Fate hath prouided for thee,

You were a Mayde, sweare still, y'are no worse now,
I left you as I found you, haue I startled you,
I am quit wth you now for my discouerie
Youre Outcryes and youre cunnings, farewell Brokage!

    Wh. Qs. p. Naye, staye and heare mee but giue thanks a litle, *70*
If youre Eare can endure a worke so gratious,
Then you maye take youre pleasure,

    Bl. Bs. p. I haue don that;

    Wh. Qs. p. That power that hath preserud me from this
      Deuill

    Bl. Bs. p. How!   *75*

    Wh. Qs. p. This, that maye challenge the cheif chayre in hell
And sitt aboue his Master,

    Bl. Bs. p. Bring in merit!

    Wh. Qs. p. That sufferdst him through blinde Lust to bee lead,
Last night to the Action of some Common bed;   *80*

    Bl. Qs. p. [*Intus*] Not ouercommon neyther!

    Bl. Bs. p. Hah, what voyce is that;

    Wh. Qs. p. Of Virgins bee thou euer honored:
Now you maye goe, you heare I haue giuen thankes Sir,

    Bl. Bs. p. Here's a strange game, did not I lye wth you?   *85*

    Intus. Noh!

    Bl. Bs. p. What a deuill art thou

    Wh. Qs. p. I will not answere you sir,
After thanksgiuing;

    Bl. Bs. p. Why you made a promise to mee   *90*
After the Contract;

    Intus. Yes;

    Bl. Bs. p. A pox confound thee
I speake not to thee—and you were præparde for't,
And sett youre Joyes more high,   *95*

    Intus.—Then you could reach, Sir;

    Bl. Bs. p. Light, tis a bawdie Voyce I'le slit the throate ont,
                            Enter Bl. Qs. p.

    Bl. Qs. p. What? offer Violence to youre bedfellowe?
To one that workes so kindlie, wthout Rape?

    Bl. Bs. p. My bedfellowe?   *100*

Bl. Qs. p. Do you plant youre Scorne agaynst me?
Why when I was probationer at Bruxells
That Engine was not knowne, then Adoration
Fild up the place and Wonder was in fashion
105 I'st turnd to the wilde Seede of Contempt so soone?
Can 5 yeares stampe a Bawde, praye looke uppon mee
I haue youth ynough to take it, tis no more
Since you were cheife Agent for the Transportation
Of ladies daughters, if you bee remembred,
110 Some of theire portions I could name, who purst em too
They were soone dispossest of worldlie Cares
That came into youre fingers;
    Bl. Bs. p. Shall I heare her?
    Bl. Qs. p. Holie Derision yes, till thy Eare swells
115 Wth thy owne Venom, thy prophane lifes Vomit;
Whose Neice was shee you poysond wth childe, twice,
Then gaue her out possest wth a fowle Spirit
When twas indeed youre Bastard;
    Bl. Bs. p. I am taken   *Enter white Bs. p.*
120 In myne owne Toyles;   *and white Queene*
    Wh. Bs. p. Yes, and tis iust you should bee;
    Wh. Q. And thou lewde pawne the shame of Womanhood:
    Bl. Bs. p. I'me lost of all hands,
    Bl. Qs. p. And I cannot feele
125 The weight of my perdition now hees taken,
T'as not the Burden of a Grasshopper,
    Bl Bs. p. Thou whore of Order, Cockatrice in Voto;
                           Enter Bl: Kts. p.
    Bl. Kts. p. Yond's the White Bishop's pawne, haue at his
    heart now,
    Wh. Qs. p. Hold Monster-Impudence, wouldst thou heape
    a murder
130 On thy first fowle attempt, oh merciles Blood-hound,
Tis time that thou wert taken;
    Bl. Kts. p. Death! preuented!
    Wh. Qs. p. For thy sake, and yond partner in thy shame,
Ile neuer knowe man farder, then by name.   *exeunt.*

Enter Bl. K. Q, Duke, Bl. Kt. wth   [v, iii.]
              the white Kt and his Duke

Wh. Kt. Y'aue both enricht my knowledge, (Royall Sir)
And my Content together;
    Bl. K. Stead of Riot
Wee sett you onelie welcome, Surfet is
A thing thats seldome heard of in these parts;   5
    Wh. Kt. I heare of the more Vertue when I misse on't,
    Bl. Kt. Wee do not use to burie in our Bellyes
2 hundred thousand ducketts and then boast on't,
Or exercize the ould Roman paynfull-Idlenes
Wth care of fetching Fishes far from home,   10
The Golden-headed Coracine out of Ægipt
The Salpa from Eleusis, or the pelamis
Wch some call Summer-Whiting from Calcedon,
Salmons from Aquitayne, Helops from Rhodes,
Cockles from Chios, franckt and fatted up   15
Wth Far and Sapa flower and cockted wine,
Wee cramb no birds, nor Epicurean-like
Enclose some Creekes of the Sea, as Sergius Crata did
Hee that inuented the first Stewes for Oysters
And other Sea-Fish, who beside the pleasure   20
Of his owne throate
Got large Reuennewes by th' Inuentiŏ,
Whose Fat Example the Nobilitie followed;
Nor do wee imitate that arch-Gurmundizer,
Wth 2 and twentye Courses at one Dinner,   25
And betwixt euerie Course hee and his Guesse
Wash't and usde weomen then sate downe and strenghtnd;
Lust swimming in theire Dishes, wch no sooner
Was tasted but was readie to bee Vented,
    Wh. Kt. Most Impious Epicures!   30
    Bl. Kt. Wee commend rather
Of 2 Extreames the parsimonie of pertinax
Who had halfe Lettices sett up to serue agen,
Or his Successor Julian that would make

35 3 Meales of a Leane Hare, and often supp
  Wth a greene Figg, and wipe his Beard as wee can;
  The ould bewaylers of Excesse in those dayes,
  Complayn'd there was more coyne bid for a Cooke
  Then for a warhorse, but now Cookes are purchasd
40 After the Rate of Triumphs, and some dishes
  After the Rate of Cookes, wch must needs make
  Some of youre whitehouse Gurmundizers, spetiallie
  Youre wealthie plumpe plebeians, like the Hogs
  Wch Scalliger cites, that could not moue for Fat,
45 So insensible of eyther Prick or Goade,
  That Mice made Holes to Needle in theire buttocks
  And they nere felt em; there was once a Ruler
  Cyrene's Gouernor, choakte wth his owne paunch
  Wch death Fat Sanctius K. of Castile fearing
50 Through his infinite Masse of Bellie, rather chose
  To bee kild suddenlie, by a pernitious herbe
  Taken to make him Leane, wch ould Corduba
  K. of Morocco counseld his feare to
  Then hee would hazard to bee stunck to death
55 As that huge Cormorant that was choakte before him;
    Wh. Kt. Well, you're as sound a Spokesman (Sr) for
        parsimony
  Cleane Abstinence, and scarce one meale a daye,
  As euer spake wth tongue,
    Bl. K. Censure him mildlie, Sir,
60 Twas but to finde discourse
    Bl. Q. Hee'le rayse of anie thing
    Wh. Kt. I shall bee halfe afrayde to feede hereafter
    Wh. D. Or I beshrewe my heart, for I feare Fatnes
  The Fogg of Fatnes, as I feare a Dragon,
65 The comlines I wish for thats as glorious;
    Wh. Kt. Youre course is wondrous strickt, I should
        transgresse sure,
  Were I to change my side, as you haue much wrought mee
      to it:
    Bl. Kt. How you misprize, this is not meant to youward

You that are woond up to the height of Feeding
By Clime and Custome are dispencst wthall;   *70*
You maye eate Kid, Cabrito, Calfe and Ton's
Eate, and eate euerie daye, twice if you please,
Naye the Franckt Hen, fattend wth milke and Corne
A Riot wch the Inhabitants of Delos
Were first Inuenters of, or the Crambd Cockle   *75*
  Wh. Kt. Well, for the Foode, Ime happilie resolude on,
But for the Diet of my disposition
There comes a trouble, you will hardlie finuͨ
Foode to please that;
  Bl. Kt. It must bee a strange Nature   *80*
Wee cannot finde a dish for, hauing policie
The Mr-Cooke of Christendome to dresse it,
Praye name youre Natures dyet,
  Wh. Kt. The first Messe
Is hott Ambition!   *85*
  Bl. Kt. That's but serude in puff paste,
Alasse the meanest of our Cardinalls Cookes
Can dresse that dinner, youre Ambition, Sir,
Can fetch no farder compasse then the World?
  Wh. Kt. Thats certayne Sir,   *90*
  Bl. Kt. Wee're about that alreadie;
And in the large Feast of our Vast Ambition
Wee count but the White Kingdome whence you came from
The garden for our Cooke to pick his Salletts:
The Foode's leane France larded wth Germanie,   *95*
Before wch comes the Graue—Chast Seigniorie
Of Venice, serude in Capon-like in whitebroath,
From our cheife Ouen, Italie, the Bakemeates,
Sauoye, the Salt, Geneua, the Chipt Manchet,
Belowe the Salt the Netherlands are placst   *100*
A Common dish at Lower end ath Table
For meaner pride to fall to, for our second Course
A Spit of portugalls serude in for plouers
Indians and Moores for Blackbirds, all this while
Holland stands readie melted, to make Sawce   *105*

On all Occasions, when the Voyder comes
And wth such cheere our Crambd Hopes wee suffize,
Zealand sayes Grace, for fashion, then wee rize:
    Wh. Kt. Heeres Meate ynough a conscience for Ambition!
110   *Bl. Kt.* If there bee anye want, there's Switzerland,
Polonia, and such pickled things will serue
To furnish out the Table;
    Wh. Kt. You saye well, Sir;
But heres the miserie, when I haue stopt the mouth
115 Of one Vice, there's another gapes for Foode,
I am as Couetous as a Barren Wombe
The Graue, or what's more rauennous,
    Bl. Kt. Wee are for you Sir;
Call you that haynous thats good husbandrie,
120 Why wee make monye of our fayths, our prayers
Wee make the uerie death bed buy her Comforts,
Most deerelie paye for all her pious Counsells,
Leaue rich Reuennues for a fewe Sale-Orisons
Or else they passe unreconcilde wthout em,
125 Did you but View the Vaults wthin our Monasterie,
You'de sweare then, Plutus wch the Fiction calls
The Lord of Riches were entombd wthin 'em;
    Bl. D. You cannot passe for Tuns!
    Wh. Kt. Ist possible;
130   *Wh. D.* But how shall I bestowe the Vice I bring (Sirs)
You quite forgett mee, I shall bee lockt out
By youre strickt key of Life;
    Bl. Kt. Is youres so fowle (Sir)
    Wh. D. Some that are pleasde to make a Wanton on't
135 Call it infirmitie of bloud, Flesh-Frayltie,
But certayne theres a worse Name in youre bookes for't;
    Bl. Kt. The Trifle of all Vices, the meere Innocent,
The uerie Nouice of this house of Claye: Venerie!
If I but hugg thee hard I showe the worst on't,
140 Tis all the fruite wee haue here after Supper;
Naye, at the Ruines of a Nunnerie once
6 thousand Infants heads found in a fishpond,

Wh. Kt. How!

Bl. Kt. How? I how? how came they thether thinke you?
Huldrick Bishop of Ausburge in his Epistle   *145*
To Nicholas the first can tell you how,
Maye bee hee was at clensing of the Pond;
I can but smile to thinke how it would puzzle
All Mother-Maydes that euer liude in those parts
To knowe theire owne childes head, but is this all?   *150*

Bl. D. Are you ours yet?

Wh. Kt. One more, and I am silencst,
But this that comes now will diuide us questionlesse,
Tis ten times ten times worse then the Forerunners,

Bl. Kt. Is it so uilde there is no name ordaynde for't   *155*
Toades haue theire Titles, and Creation gaue
Serpents and Adders those names to bee knowne by

Wh. Kt. This of all others beares the hiddenst Venom
The smoothest poyson,—I am an Arch-Dissembler S^r,

Bl. Kt. How!   *160*

Wh. Kt. Tis my Natures Brand turne from mee, Sir,
The time is yet to come that ere I spake
What my heart mean't!

Bl. Kt. And call you that a Vice,
Auoyde all prophanation I beseech you   *165*
The onelie prime State-Virtue uppon earth
The policie of Empires, oh take heede, Sir,
For feare it take displeasure and forsake you,
It is a Jewell of that prætious Value
Whose worth's not knowen but to the skillfull Lapidarie,   *170*
The Instrument that picks ope princes hearts,
And locks up ours from them wth the same Motion;
You neuer yet came neere our soules till now,
Now y'are a Brother to us, what wee haue donne
Has beene dissemblance euer,   *175*

Wh. Kt. There you lye then
And the Games ours—wee giue thee Checkmate by
Discouerye, King, the Noblest Mate of all;   *A great shout*

Bl. K. I'me lost, Ime taken.   *and flourish*

180   *Wh. Kt.* Ambitious, Couetous, luxurious Falshood
       Wh. D. Dissembler includes all,
       Bl. K. All hopes confounded,
       Bl. Q. Miserable Condition!

                                           Enter White King
                                           Q, white pawnes
       Wh. K. Oh let mee blesse mine Armes wth this deere treasure,
185 Truths glorious Masterpeice, see, Queene of Sweetnes,
       Hee's in my bosome safe, and yond fayre Structure
       Of Comlie honor, his true-blest Assistant,
       Wh. Q. Maye theire Integrities euer possesse
       That peacefull Sanctuarie,
190   *Wh. Kt.* As twas a Game (Sir)
       Wun wth much hazard, so wth much more triumph
       Wee gaue him Check-Mate by discouerie Sir;
       Wh. K. Obscuritie is now the fittest fauour
       Falshood can sue for, it well suites perdition
195 Tis theire best course that so haue lost theire fame
       To putt theire heads into the Bagg for Shame,
       And there behold the Baggs Mouth, like Hell opens
       To take her due, and the lost Sonnes appeare   *The Bagge*
       Greedilie gaping for Encrease of Fellowship   *opens, the Bl.*
200 In Infamie, the last desire of Wretches,   *Side in it.*
       Aduancing theire perdition-branded foreheads
       Like Enuies Issue, or a Bed of Snakes:
       Bl. Bs. p. See, all's confounded, the Game's lost, Kings taken,
       Fat. B. The whitehouse has giuen us the Bag I thanke em
205   *Jesting p.* They had neede haue giuen you a whole Bagg by
                    youre selfe,
       Sfoote, this Fat Bishop has so squelcht and squeezde mee,
       So ouerlayd mee, I haue no Vergis left in mee,
       You shall finde all my goodnes and you looke for't
       In the bottome of the Bagg;
210   *F. B.* Thou malapert Pawne!
       The Bishop must haue Roome, hee will haue roome,
       And roome to lye at pleasure
          Jest. p. All the bagg I thinke

Is roome too scant for youre Spoletta-Paunch,

   Bl. Bs. p. Downe Viper of our Order, art thou showing   *215*

Thy impudent-whorish Front,

   Bl. Qs. p. Yes, Monster Holines

   Wh. Kt. Contention in the pitt is Hell diuided

   Wh. K. You'de neede haue some of Maiestie and power,

To keepe good rule amongst you, make Roome Bishop,   *220*

   F. B. I am not so easilie moude when I'me once sett,

I scorne to stir for anie King on earth

   Wh. Q. Here comes the Queene what saye you then to her?

   F. B. Indeed a Queene maye make a Bishop stir:

   Wh. Kt. Roome for the mightiest Machiauill polititian,   *225*

That ere the Deuill hatcht of a Nuns Egg:

   F. B. Heele peck a Hole ith Bagg and gett out shortly

But I'me sure I shall bee the last creepes out,

And thats the miserie of Greatnes euer,

Foh, youre polititian is not sound ith Vent   *230*

I smell him hether,

   Wh. D. Roome for a sunburnt Tanzye facst beloude

An Oliue-Colourd Ganimed, and thats all

Thats worth the Bagging;

   F. B. Crowde in all you can   *235*

The Bishop will bee still uppermost Man

Maugrë King, Queene, or polititian;

   Wh. K. So, now lett the Bagg close, the fittest Wombe

For trecherie pride and malice whilst wee winner-like

Destroying (through heauens power) what would destroy   *240*

Welcome our White Knight wth Lowde peales of Joye

                                ex—t

Finis

A Game at Chesse

EPILOGUE

Wh: Queenes pawne.

My Mistris the White Queene hath sent mee forth
And bade mee bowe thus lowe to all of Worth
That are true Frends of the White House, & cause
Wch shee hopes most of this Assemblie drawes
5   For anie else by Enuies Marke denoted
To those night-Glow-wormes in the Bagg deuoted
Where e're they sit, stand, and in Corners lurke
They'le bee soone knowen by theire deprauing worke:
But shees assurde what they'de committ to Bayne
10   Her white Frends loues will build up fayre agayne:

TEXTUAL NOTES

T—Trinity MS.
B—Bridgewater-Huntington MS.
I—first bad quarto.

L—Lansdowne MS. (No. 690).
M—Malone MS. (No. 25).
II—second bad quarto.

III—good quarto.

No attempt has been made to catalogue all the many and gross errors of the quartos. *M* has no stage-directions except those mentioned in these notes.

THE PICTURE PLAINLY EXPLAINED

Found only in I and II. Whether or not Middleton was the author it is impossible to say.

LINES TO MR WILLIAM HAMMOND

Found only in M.

PROLOGUE

The Prologue is omitted in M. In L it is inserted between the Induction and the beginning of Act I.

INDUCTION

page 51

Ignatius Loyola appearing…: *so T, B, I, II;* Enter Ignatius (discovering Errour sleeping): *III;* Ignatius Loyola and Error: *L, M.* **5.** institutions: *I, II.* **14.** and founder: *B.* **15.** saluted by 'em: *I, II;* 7 yeares: *B.* **18.** saluted me: *I, II.* **19.** not roome: *B.* **23.** Letts: *T, B, I, II.* **27.** Sicelie and Ursula: *L, M, III.* **28.** the: *omitted in B.*

page 52

32. too, trust mee: *I, II.* **41.** eye *is inserted above the line in T in another hand.* **42.** What Game prethee?: *L, M, III.* **53.** *the stage-direction is from III; it is omitted in T, B, I, II. L has* Enter yᵉ white House & yᵉ Black (as in order of the Game). **57.** of all the Game: *B.* **60.** Corruptedly: *III.* **65.** Thy: *all the texts but T.*

page 53

67. light performents: *I, II.* **68.** nor worthie: *III.* **75.** against the Game: *I, II.* **79.** rulde in by one: *I, II.* **80.** and view 'em: *I, II.* **83.** Exeunt *added at the end in L, M, III.*

I. i.

L, M, III have Exeunt *at the end of the Induction, and at the beginning of this scene L has* Enter yᵉ white-Queenes Pawne, & yᵉ Black Queenes-Pawne; *III has* Enter severally, White Queenes Pawne, and Black-Queenes Pawne; *M has* The white-Queenes, & yᵉ Black-Queenes

A Game at Chesse

Pawnes. Then yᵉ Black Bishop's Pawne. Then yᵉ Whi: Bishops Pawne & yᵉ Bl. Knights Pawne, Then yᵉ Black-Knight, Then ye wh. King's Pawne. **5.** in that not ours: *I, II*; in that shee is not ours: *B.* **8.** Theis are: *L.* **11–15.** *omitted in M.*

page 54

15. Eies: *III.* **22.** firme: *III.* **27.** that heate: *I, II.* **30.** flied: *B.* **31.** eyes: *I, II.* **33.** a Jesuite *(in stage-direction) omitted in L, I, II, III.* **35.** Will make: *L, M, III.* **41.** But the heart (Lady): *L, M, III.* **45.** E'ene in his armes, in his owne bosom: *I, II.* **46.** Jesuitesse: *B, I, II.* **47.** worth and greatnesse: *B, I, II.*

page 55

53–68. *omitted in M.* **53.** these in voto: *I, II.* **60.** the noble: *III.* **66.** Often times: *I, II.* **67.** Of States: *III.* **75.** Do you: *L, M, III.* **76.** Exit: *L.* **78–80.** *omitted in M.* **85.** Praise, lies like a Pearle: *L.* **86.** from opening: *I, II.*

page 56

89. delightfull: *B, I, II.* **97.** the good worke: *I, II, III.* **102.** deasires: *B.* **103.** It's easily: *I, II.* **113.** Who so innocent: *B, I, II; Who's: L.* **120–124.** *omitted in M.* **120.** by discouering: *B.*

page 57

126. your discouerie: *I, II.* **127–131.** to bee nice...past Cure: *omitted in M.* **130.** that Tumor: *I, II.* **133.** now: *omitted in L, M, III.* **135.** Night Counsels: *III*; yours might counsell: *I, II.* **136.** any account: *I, II.* **144.** for truths safety: *I, II.* **145.** some sinful, some sound: *I, II*; some sound, some sinful: *III.* **154.** cleerer: *B.*

page 58

161. shut up: *L.* **163.** slip of grace: *III.* **169.** the Competitor: *I, II*; his competitors: *III.* **174–177.** *omitted in M.* **178.** it seemes you: *I, II.* **179.** *omitted in I, II.* **180.** which: *L*; in the ends: *I, II.* **184.** must confesse: *B, L, M, I, II, III.* **189–200.** *omitted in M.* **194.** exact in all things: *B.* **196.** wishes: *B, I, II.*

page 59

200. workes glory: *I, II.* **202–205.** *omitted in M.* **210.** a speciall: *III.* **212.** *the stage-direction here comes after* 208 *in III, and after* 210–211 *in L, I, II.* **212.** *omitted in I, II.* **214.** yond blessed spring, but I know: *I, II.* **217–222.** wch, so long...possesse her: *omitted in M.* **222.** I, would marrie: *L*; Il'd marry: *III.* **225.** white Bishops pawne: *B.* **227.** by this hand: *omitted in L.* **232.** I haue been guiltie: *L, M, III.*

page 60

234. memory of it: *I, II.* **238.** most noble Lady: *M.* **239–246.** *omitted in M.* **242.** they're out of: *L, M, III.* **245.** the leprosie: *I, II.* **247.** youre divell: *I, II.* **248.** eye: *B.* **251.** Fellon: *B, L, M, III.* **254.** one Condition: *B.* **256.** no peace: *I, II.* **257.** acquittance: *I, II.* **258.** difference: *I, II.* **260.** It is Noblenes: *L.* **261.** Exit: *L.* **262.** instruct you throughly: *III.* **267.** Intelligencies: *L*; intelligencers: *I, II.* **269.** and one: *L, M, III.*

page 61

272–274. line-arrangement in *T :* the great worke...Monarchie nor/ Hierarchie...lesse (*two lines only*). **273.** Divine: *III.* **274.** I brag less: *I, II.* **275.** But I have: *L, M, III*; of 'em: *L.* **276–277.** *omitted in M.* **276.** father: *B.* **277.** Yea, and: *L, M, III.* **285.** mischief: *I, II, III.* **289.** (Especially in privat): *M.* **290.** *omitted in L;* Cherie Guarden: *B.* **291.** are not: *M.* **292.** be with you: *M.* **301.** these great ones: *I, II*; this Guytinens: *III.* **305.** Pupills: *I, II.* **306.** trifle gone: *I, II.*

page 62

307. good game: *I, II.* **308.** pawne in: *L, M, III.* **310–313.** linearrangement in *T :* I you hold...youre/playe...youde plye/the Game... priuate) (*three lines only*). **312.** your Game: *L.* **314.** the great worke the maine existence: *B.* **318.** So you may deny: *I, II.* **320.** Cedars: *I, II.* **327.** Looke, there's: *III.* **330.** I thinke: *L, M, III.* **331.** this Italica: *L, M, III.* **332.** they have put: *L, M, III.* **333.** there: *I, II.* **334.** blind work this: *I, II.* **338.** leave your jesting: *I, II.* **339.** owne name: *L, M, III.* **340.** the wh. Kings pawne: *omitted in I, II.* **342.** owne (Sir): *B.*

page 63

344. indeed pretiously: *I, II.* **345.** You see my outside, but not my heart: *I, II*; heart, Sir: *B.* **346.** Intelligences: *L.* **347.** ripenesse: *I, II.* **351.** Pursse or Powre: *M.* **353.** raise strength against: *L, M*; raise strength 'gainst: *III.* **354.** no longer: *L, M, III.* **355.** iealious: *L, III.* **357.** Fleece of Gold: *I, II.* **360.** which way: *L, M, I, II, III.*

II. i.

Stage-direction: Enter White Queenes Pawne, reading: *III*; Enter yᵉ white-Queenes-Pawne (reading) & to her, the Black Bishop's Pawne: *L*; The White Queenes Pawne (reading) The Black Bˢ Pawne, Then yᵉ Black-Queenes-Pawne. Then yᵉ Black-Bishop, & Black-Knight: *M.* **3.** expostulations: *I, II*; expostulation or exception: *B.* **4.** heard of: *I, II.* **6.** lies gently reconciled: *I, II*; 'tis latelie: *III.* **8.** *stage-direction omitted in L.* **9–29.** *omitted in M.*

page 64

14. *omitted in III;* subscribed: *B;* the letter: *omitted in L, III.* **15.** immeasurably: *II.* **18.** at this time: *B.* **27.** has taken: *B.* **30.** rule of the: *I, II.* **31.** Prescription: *L, M, I, II.* **32.** that alacritie: *III.* **33.** Her eyes move: *III*; Letter: *I, II.* **37–47.** *omitted in M.* **41–43.** linearrangement in *T :* Boundlesse...of all/duties...Goodnes (*two lines only*). **43.** Well set her: *I, II*; Well here I set: *III.*

123

page 65
46. farre: *I, II*. **53.** then: *omitted in B*. **57.** lips: *I, II, III*. **59.** and so little: *III*. **63–70.** bee more...best (Sir): *omitted in M*. **64.** most like: *III*. **68.** owne Cause: *L*. **73–81.** *omitted in M*. **75.** It flies abroad from these lips dealt in parcels: *I, II*. **80.** looke of: *B, L, I, II*.

page 66
87–88. *the order of these two lines is reversed in I, II*. **88.** if vertue: *B*. **94–98.** is this...forgot: *omitted in M. An Alexandrine is the result*. **98.** They last they most forget: *I, II*. **101–111.** *omitted in M*. **103.** forwards: *I, II*. **110.** come come neerer: *B*. **112.** Was that in scorne: *I, II*. **113.** prooued: *B, I, II*. **114.** great Monarchy: *I, II*. **115.** flye abroad: *I, II*; spread abroad: *III*. **117.** threatnens: *T*; He threatens me: *M*. **118–124.** *omitted in M*. **118–119.** *Line-arrangement in T :* that should/helpe mee, I....

page 67
119. of my fayth: *B*; I was never: *III*. **124.** neerer the offarer: *B*; neerer the offerors: *I, II*; to the Officer: *III*. **128–134.** my respect... Oh heauen!: *omitted in M*. **130.** the repulse: *III*. **132.** so *omitted in B, L, I, II, III*. **133.** too great: *III*. **137.** thy Love: *L*. **139–148.** *omitted in M*. **143.** make me none: *III*. **146.** dost weepe: *I, II*. **151.** sir *omitted in L, M*. **152.** for to guide me to: *I, II*. **153.** Iue uowde: *T, B*. **154.** mee *omitted in I, II*; reiect: *III*. **155.** Noise within *after this line in III*.

page 68
156–159. *omitted in M*. **158.** most Princes: *L, M, III*. **160.** confound noyse: *so all MSS. and Qq. As Bullen pointed out, part of the original stage-direction has crept into the text. T, L, and M all have the direction at the end of this line; in I and II it comes after* 159, *while B has a* noyse *after* 161. **161.** *omitted in M*. **162.** I'll: *M*; danger: *B*; on all dangers: *I, II*. **163–166.** *omitted in M*. **165.** who being: *B*. **167.** and will: *M*; the Arch-hypocrite: *I, II*. **168.** Exit: *found only in III, which also adds* Noyse within. **169–170.** *all one line in T and B*. **171.** *stage-direction omitted in T*. **174.** *omitted in M*. **175–176.** *line-arrangement in T :* wrought her/plyant, I.... **177.** on purpose: *L, M, III*; of purpose: *I, II*. **178.** ends: *I, II*. **179–183.** *omitted in M*. **181.** *omitted in I, II*. **184.** yonder: *omitted in B, I, II*. **186.** cheekes, till they: *L, M, III*. **187–190.** *omitted in M*.

page 69
189. yeares: *B, L*; I have seaven yeares: *I, II*. **193–199.** *omitted in M*. **194.** Motto still: *B, I, II*. **196.** all Nations: *III*; on a: *I, II*. **198.** trymer, and fresher: *I, II*; Vessells...Barkes: *B, III*. **201.** *omitted in B, M, I, II*. **203.** one of his Society: *I, II*. **205.** Be it thus then: *M*. **207.** *omitted in T*. **208.** at our house: *I, II*. **209.** at least past: *B*. **210–212.** *omitted in M. A broken line results*. **212.** thy Journey: *I, II, III*.

213. *line-arrangement in T:* Sir,/how for... **217.** *omitted in M.* **219.** *omitted in M.* **220.** Intelligencies: *L, III.* **221.** rather: *omitted in I, II.* **223–224.** *omitted in M.*

page 70

226. 'hath...Intelligencies: *L.* **227–229.** *omitted in M.* **227.** 'hath: *L;* he hath: *III.* **228.** the names: *I, II.* **231.** by this light: *III;* Anglica: most of these: *L, M.* **232.** *omitted in M;* of 'em: *I, II;* of them: *L, III.* **234.** the safe: *III.* **237.** these three from: *I, II;* These from: *L, M, III.* **238.** (go Jesuitesse): *I, II.* **241.** an exceeding: *I, II.* **242.** sir: *omitted in L.* **243.** the Kingdome: *I, II.* **246.** fits my humour: *III.* **250.** Oh no familiar: *I;* Oh no familiarity: *II.* **251.** and subteller: *omitted in I, II.* **252.** scortch mee: *T;* scorch em: *I, II;* scorch 'em me: *L, M, III.* **252–262.** burne 'em...bid you, pawne: *omitted in M.* **255.** strangelye: *omitted in B.* **258.** came spectacl'd: *III.* **260.** pick their: *I, II.* **262.** *L and III have* Exit *at the end of this line.*

page 71

264. *M omits the rest of this scene, and has* Exeunt *at the end of this line.* **265.** *no stage-direction in B.* **276.** Come help me with: *L, III.* **277.** *omitted in B, I, II.* **281.** Tis not much troubled with mirth, Sir: *B, I, II.*

II. ii.

Headed: Scᵃ 2ᵃ: *L, M;* Scena Secunda: *III. Stage-direction:* with his pawne: *I, II;* and his Pawne: *L, III.* The Fat-Bishop & his Pawne: Then yᵉ Bl. Bᵖ. & Bl. Knight. Then yᵉ Wh. & Bl. Houses (severally): *M.* **3.** but greatly holy: *B, I, II.* **5.** often leane: *I, II.* **8.** but for the pure part: *I, II;* but the purer part: *B.* **9.** That's at: *I, II.* **10.** from a huge: *I, II.* **11–12.** *omitted in M.* **12.** to bed: *I, II, III.* **13.** Invective: *III;* my last Inuectiues: *the beginning of Middleton's handwriting for a page in B.* **15.** publication, Sir: *B.* **16.** Sir: *omitted in B.*

page 72

19. *M has* Goe, be-gon *added to l. 18 instead of this line. The stage-direction is omitted in B, I, II, III.* **20–47.** *omitted in B, which has* Enter Bl. Kt. *after l. 19.* **21.** Set, eate, and drinke: *I, II.* **23–29.** *omitted in L.* **25–34.** *omitted in M.* **27.** slit the roote: *I, II.* **29–30.** *all one line in T.* **32.** black-house: *I, II.* **33.** time to revolt: *I, II.* **34.** to say truth: *I, II.* **35.** But I...: *M.* **41.** *omitted in M.* **42.** much more drab: *I.* **44–47.** *omitted in M.* **48.** *stage-direction omitted in T.* **50.** when hee did: *B.* **51.** vouchsafe: *B.* **52.** he found: *B;* there: *omitted in I, II.*

page 73

55. *stage-direction omitted in III.* **56.** *in B l. 78 is inserted between ll. 56 and 57 in smaller writing.* **57.** turne coate: *omitted in I, II.* **58.** h'as wrought our house: *B.* **61.** *B omits from this line to the end of the scene.* **63–67.** And then dam...alreadie: *omitted in M.* **65.** aduerse part: *T;* feeds on: *I, II.* **68.** Phisick he prescribd: *L, M.* **69.** Surgeon he

A Game at Chesse

provided: *L, M*. **70.** tell thee: *III*; uncutholicall: *I, II*. **77.** Oh: *omitted in L, M*; Oh Insufferable: *omitted in I, II, but the next speech is given to* B. B. *instead of* Bl. Kt. **78–82.** *line-arrangement in T :* Ile...of the/ churches...tosse him, hee/lookes...drinck/and Vrine.... **79–82.** hee lookes...write: *omitted in M*. **82.** second bishops dead: *I, II*. **84–85.** *omitted in M*. **85.** rests in: *I, II*.

page 74

89–91. *omitted in M*. **93.** *omitted in M ; stage-direction omitted in I, II;* Enter yᵉ white-House & yᵉ Black-House (sevrally): *L*; Enter Kin. Qu. Kni. Duke, Bishops of both sides, and Pawnes: *III*. **98.** and boldnesse: *III*. **99.** *omitted in III*. **99–100.** *arrangement of lines :* I must ...the foole/till now: *T*; I must...plaid/: *L, M, I, II*. **102–106.** *omitted in M*. **104.** the better latain: *I, II*. **105.** plauge: *T*; Out on: *L*; Out of: *I, II*. **107.** Here, more anger yet: *I, II*. **108.** *omitted in M ; I and II have* Enter both Houses *after this line*. **109–110.** *line-arrangement in T :* Is...our/person...Deiection. **111–112.** sorrowe...wth her: *omitted in M*. **119.** terrour: *III*. **120.** of all Christendome: *I, II*. **121.** absolute: *I, II*.

page 75

127. *omitted in L, M*. **131–151.** *omitted in M*. **134.** to be at: *II*. **137–138.** *line-arrangement in T :* when wee...mens com-/panies,... there. **140.** Quits us of wounds: *III*. **142.** *omitted in I, II*. **144.** all number: *I, II*. **151.** *omitted in I, II*. **156.** scarde him: *I, II*. **157–177.** *omitted in M*. **157.** this Order: *III*. **158.** on the Earth: *I, II*.

page 76

163. Be not thou: *I, II*. **165.** Spake with: *I, II*. **169.** yeare after: *I, II*. **170–173.** *omitted in L*. **173.** and the Game: *III*. **175.** and respect: *II*. **176.** Lord Duke: *I, II*. **178–195.** if wth all speede... treads in: *omitted in M*. **184.** the more: *I, II*. **188.** no roome: *III*. **190.** how you can: *I, II*. **192.** all blood-threats that thunder: *I, II*. **194.** Crafts: *III*; Trust: *I, II*. **196.** and playe: *M*.

page 77

199. *omitted in II*. **199–205.** *omitted in M*. **201.** will she have it: *I, II*. **202.** the more unclean: *I, II*. **203.** and impious: *I, II*; and most impious: *III*. **206.** haples Evening: *L*; Yesterday: *III*. **207–218.** *omitted in M*. **222.** treachery: *I, II*. **227.** *omitted in M ; attributed to* W.K. *in L*. **229.** *omitted in M*. **230.** Wh. Kni,: *III*.

page 78

235. Wh. Kni.: *III*. **235–239.** *omitted in M*. **242.** *omitted in M ;* Oh, sir, indeede: *I, II*. **244.** easilie *and* you maye trust to it: *omitted in M*. **248–250.** *line-arrangement in T :* how...so good/to holines...rather (*two lines only*). **248.** they were in one: *I, II*. **250.** That I ever: *L*. **254.** Wh. Kni.: *III*; where sets: *I, II*. **258.** my frend: *T*; leaves: *I, II*.

260. art thou so left: *III*; friendlesse Innocence: *I, II*. **262.** Wh. K.: *III*. **266.** chiefely: *I, II*. **269.** her: *omitted in I, II; the stage-direction is omitted in I, II, III, but inserted in M*. **270–271.** *omitted in M*.

page 79

271. the Galician braine: *I, II*. **272.** upon like: *I, II*. **275–280.** *omitted in M*. **277.** virginities the: *I, II*. **281.** Bl. Bish.: *III*. **285.** the twelve: *I, II*. **286.** not so much...pommel see: *I, II*. **294.** *I, II omit* Exeunt, *but have* Finit Actus Secundus.

III. i.

Incipit Tertius: *I, II*; Actus Tertius, Scena Prima: *L, M, III*. *Stage-direction:* The Fat Bishop: Then the Bl. K^t Then his Pawne Then ye white & Black-Houses (severally): *M; in B* Enter fat Bishop *is altered in Middleton's hand to* The Fat Bishop, *and so becomes merely a speech-heading, following on after* II. ii. 60. **2.** writ: *I, II*. **3–5.** *omitted in M*. **5.** Orifice: *B*. **6.** gap'd for: *B, III*; I ha' gapte fort: *omitted in L, M*; I have got: *I, II*.

page 80

7–11. *omitted in M*. **9.** would fit: *I, II*. **13.** disease-bred honour: *I, II*. **20.** Maister-peece: *I, II*. **25.** youre most reuerend: *B*. **27–32.** *omitted in M*. **32.** *III has the stage-direction:* Hee reades the Letter; *L and M have the speech-heading:* fat B. reades; *in T there is only the heading* the Letter, *and it is not assigned to F. B. although in B at l. 33 it is so assigned. Neither T nor B has a speech-heading at l. 46, although both have one at l. 49*. **33.** meaning me: *B, L, M, I, II, III*. **34.** *omitted in M*. **36.** prooves the onely cause of your ill fortune at this time: *I, II*. **39.** *The dashes in this line and l. 41 are not in T; they are added, on the analogy of those in l. 33, from B;* how? had it so?: *B, M;* at my next: *B*. **39–41.** wch by...Supremacie: *omitted in M*.

page 81

42. hah! all my bodies bloud mounts up to Face: *B*. **45.** *no speech-heading in T, B, I, II;* Fat. Bish.: *III;* reades: *M;* fat B. reades: *L;* Thinke on't seriouslie: *omitted in M*. **47.** of youre disobedience: *omitted in M*. **53–57.** *omitted in M*. **54–55.** Two or three bitter bookes, against the White-house, | And inuenting another Recantation: *III*. **56.** I am in on th'other: *L, M, III*. **59.** Thou shalt see: *all texts but T;* shortlie: *omitted in I, II*. **62–68.** *omitted in M*. **63.** yea blood: *III*. **64.** most deare primitive: *I, II*. **65.** poynts & speares: *B*. **67.** the sonne: *I, II*. **73–74.** *omitted in M*. **74.** *omitted in L, III*. **76.** Ambitions: *B, L, M, III*. **78.** exit: *omitted in B*.

page 82

80–81. Like...Quagmire: *omitted in M*. **82.** and not shame 'em: *omitted in M*. **84.** In the remembrance: *III*. **86–91.** *omitted in M*. **87.** of the Earth: *III*. **88.** procurde a Gallant Fleete: *B, L, I, II*.

90. Pyrats: *B, L, I, II.* **94.** without touching: *I, II.* **95.** Heritiques: *III*; to this houre: *III.* **100.** coaches: *I, II*; their safe: *I, II, III.* **107–109.** *line-arrangement in T:* my Ribs to/thinke...uncensurde but/ in thought...question'd. **109.** A Whisper or a Whistle: *M.* **112.** too: *omitted in III*; had sopes too: *B*; got good soup too: *I, II.* **113.** from Countries for: *I, II.* **114.** hopd for Preferments: *I, II.*

page 83

117. Enter Bl. Kts. P.: *B*; Enter blacke Knights pawne: *I, II.* **119.** I'me so sad: *I, II.* **120–129.** *omitted in M.* **124–126.** *line-arrangement in T:* Mine? mischief...Nayle, and/a Driuer...Machiauill. *The arrangement adopted is that of L.* **132.** Three-score: *L, M, I, II*; canst tell: *omitted in B.* **133–152.** *omitted in M.* **134.** How dos: *B, I, II.* **137.** their numbers: *III*; the number: *B, L, I, II*; treble: *B, L, III.* **138.** A Globe stand: *I, II, III.* **139.** drawne with Countries: *I, II.* **141.** I scarce can: *B, I, II.* **146.** sharp Eyes...pricke out: *III.* **147.** and the Climate: *III.* **148.** And will puzzle: *I, II.* **150.** too full upon: *I, II.* **151.** neede to use: *B*; neede of: *L.*

page 84

156. *omitted in M.* **158.** it seemes: *omitted in III.* **160.** White Bishop's pawne: *B, I, II.* **161.** as a: *B.* **162.** his Busines: *B.* **163–167.** *omitted in M.* **163.** a litle: *omitted in III;* there's enow: *I, II.* **165.** *B has* Enter *opposite speech-heading* Bl. B., *and* Enter both the houses *after* l. 166; *I, II have merely* Enter both Houses; *III has* Enter both Houses severally, *and L* Enter yᵉ wh & Black-houses. **167.** the vertuous: *III.* **169–171.** Of her Malitious Adversarie: Noble chaste Knight: *all one line in M—an Alexandrine.* **169.** Adversaries: *III.* **171–173.** a Title...comprizde in: *omitted in M.* **175.** the white booke: *III.* **176.** cleere ffames: *L.* **176–177.** *omitted in M.* **179.** worthy Piece: *III.* **181–188.** Most blest...Fidelitie: *omitted in M.* **185.** Magnificence: *III*; munificency: *I, II.*

page 85

187. desert claymes: *L, M, III.* **189.** Innocency: *III.* **190.** mad'st the sufferings: *I, II.* **191.** Ile take no knowledge on't: *omitted in M.* **195–209.** lett mee alone...shroud in: *omitted in M.* **196.** 'tis all: *III*; bound too: *I, II.* **197.** whats tis: *T*; W.K.: *III.* **198.** W. Kt.: *III.* **202.** admirations: *B, III.* **203.** ship: *III.* **208.** like iust heauen: *B*; like unequall: *I, II.* **210.** Wh. Kni.: *III*; This black Knight: *L, M, I, II, III.* **211.** any answere: *I, II.* **211–214.** tis a Victorie...nothing else: *omitted in M.* **215.** false Attemptor: *M.* **217.** lines six daies: *I, II.* **220.** *B has* too much *with* rash *written above* much. **222.** This Knight: *L.* **223.** as impudence: *III.*

page 86

226. bring him in strongly agen: *I, II.* **226–227.** *line-arrangement in T:* strangelie in/agen; where.... **228.** Price: *M, III*; prize can equall: *I, II*. **229–230.** *omitted in M*. **234.** the Drum: *III*. **235.** fall downe with: *II*. **235–245.** *omitted in M*; l. 234 *is thus left incomplete.* **238.** Well: *omitted in I, II*. **244.** How ever sensure: *I, II*. **247.** most noble: *I, II*. **248–249.** *omitted in M*. **248.** here: *B*. **250.** Wh. Kni.: *III*. **253.** (Sir): *omitted in B*. **256–260.** *omitted in M*. **257.** stands: *I, II*; stood: *III*. **259.** Wh. Kni.: *III*.

page 87

269. comeforts: *B, with* pleasures *written above the line.* **272.** Have I not won: *I, II*. **274–275.** *omitted in M*. **276.** B. D.: *III*. **277.** B. K.: *III*; too hasty: *I, II*. **279.** t'entrap: *I, II*. **283.** Sir: *omitted in B*. **292.** tooke youre confidence in: *III*. **293–294.** *omitted in M*. **295.** The whitenes: *I, II*.

page 88

297–300. *stage-direction omitted in T, but found in B, I, II; L, M, III have merely:* he appeares Black underneath. **298.** Wh. K.: *III*. **299.** Wh. d.: *B*. **300–315.** *omitted in M*. **300.** Wh. Q.: *B*; this Complexion: *III*; his: *I, II*. **307–308.** *line-arrangement in T:* by the/rottennes, of.... **312.** crying sin: *III*. **318–320.** *omitted in M*. **318.** B. Ki.: *I, II*. **319.** Bl. K.: *omitted in B*; B. Kt.: *I, II*; W. Kni.: *III*. **327.** thy discovery: *II*. **332.** Wh. K.: *III*. **333.** Fat. B.: *III*; Knight: *omitted in B*. **333–334.** *omitted in M*.

page 89

334. Bl. K.: *III*. **339.** by water-gate: *I, II*. **340.** to the: *III*; Blacke house: *I, II*. **341.** W. Ki.: *I, II*; Wh. K.: *III*. **343.** *stage-direction in Qq., but not in T, B*. **347–348.** *omitted in M*. **348.** wee rejoyce: *II*. **350.** prayse you: *I, II*. **351.** advancement now: *I, II*. **354.** the first way: *I, II*. **356–357.** *M omits* l. 356, *but instead has for* l. 357: No Replications: you know me well enough; replication: *I, II*. **361–362.** *line-arrangement in T:* this/daye, and.... **363.** could transcent it not: *I, II*. **367–369.** *omitted in M*. **367–370.** *omitted in B*. **368.** a rape God blesse us: *I, II*; A Rape? blesse us: *L*.

page 90

372. *omitted in M*. **373.** honest Gentleman: *III*; a Compleate one: *omitted in M*. **376–379.** *omitted in M*. **376.** Why: *omitted in I, II*; art mistaken: *I, II*; in this man: *L*. **377.** Why: *omitted in B, I, II*. **378.** all on's: *B, L, III*; all's one: *I, II*. **380.** Why: *omitted in I, II*. **389.** I cannot feele one: *I, II*. **390.** seeke the faith: *I, II*. **395.** nor: *I, II*. **397–398.** *omitted in M*. **398.** Why then observe: I'll ease you instantly: *L*; exeunt: *omitted in B, L, M*.

III. ii.

This scene is omitted in L and M, and III. iii. *follows without any break. In III this scene is headed:* Scena Secunda.

page 91

4. can be: *I, II*. **5.** prance it: *I, II*. **7.** *stage-direction omitted in I, II*; You'de looke then: *I, II*. **10.** *omitted in III*. **11.** so nigh: *I, II*.

13. Wh. p.: *omitted in T.* **16.** Naye: *omitted in I, II.* **20.** then: *omitted in I, II.* **23.** And I'll fit: *III.* **25.** Push: *B*; Pish: *I, II, III.* **25–26.** *line-arrangement in T:* I haue/whipt...and. **28.** hand: *III.* **31.** earne: *I, II.* **32.** a monthes ordinarie...will you firke: *I, II*; come sir, Friske! *B.* **35.** *omitted in I, II.* **39.** I'me glad: *I, II.*

page 92

41. And ile: *I, II.* **43.** Masse: *omitted in III.* **45.** for I can: *I, II.* **46.** Buttock: *B*; Exeunt: *omitted in I, II.*

III. iii.

Headed: Scena Tertia: *III.* **3–17.** *omitted in M.* **5–6.** *all one line in T; B has the correct line-arrangement.* **11.** vaine feares: *I, II.* **16.** enters: *I, II.* **17.** of Loues: *III.* **23–24.** *omitted in M.* **23.** that will *with second* that *omitted: I, II.* **24.** the Inuocation: *omitted in B, L, M, I, II, III.* **26.** Ægipted: *B, I, II.*

page 93

33–34. *omitted in T.* **42.** eye: *B, I, II.* **56.** *stage-direction:* enter the Bl. Bishops pawne...and stands before...: *B, I, II*; Musique. Enter the Bl. Bs. P. as in apparition richly attired: *III*; Musick yᵉ Black Bᵖˢ Pawne Enters (as in an Apparition) richelie habited: *L*; The Bl. Bᵖˢ Pawne (as in an Apparition) comes richely habited: *M.* **58.** *omitted in M.*

page 94

62. our bloods, our states: *I, II.* **63.** by fates: *I, II.* **71–72.** wch is... pleasure: *omitted in M.* **77.** *omitted in T*; exeunt: *omitted in B.*

IV. i.

L, M, III have the heading: Actus Quartus, scena prima. *Stage-direction:* Enter Black Kts. P. and Black Biˢ P.: *B, I, II*; *I, II begin the first speech thus:* Bl. Kt. P. The Jesuit in his gallant habit; *part of the stage-direction has crept into the text.* M *omits ll. 1–38, and has the following list of entrances at the head of the scene:* The Black Bᵖˢ. Pawne: and yᵉ White, & Bl: Queenes Pawnes. **2.** yeares: *B, I, II.* **6.** This a strange: *T.*

page 95

14. how! hast found: *L.* **15.** Trane of glorie: *III.* **16.** knew you: *L, III.* **17.** Catholicke: *III.* **22.** and I haue: *B.* **24–25.** *line-arrangement in T:* see his/playe, might.... **30.** ability of revenge: *I, II.* **38.** The sting: *III*; deepe: *B*; exit: *omitted in B, I, II.* **39.** apoletick Chessner: *I, II.* **41.** Oh my hart: 'tis he: *L, M.* **42.** *omitted in M.* **44.** selfe *and* Mirror: *omitted in I, II.* **45.** *T erroneously assigns this speech to* Bl. Bs. p. **47.** this fate: *I*; that fate: *II.*

page 96

52. now: *omitted in III.* **53.** *omitted in L, M.* **54.** to make: *L, M.* **60–62.** *omitted in M.* **62.** too streight: *omitted in B.* **70–73.** *omitted in*

Textual Notes

M. **71.** fortune: *B, L, I, III*; forrude: *II.* **75–78.** *omitted in M.*
78. all ready, looke into 't: *I, II*; if you would: *III*; yf you'ld: *L.*

page 97

89–101. *omitted in M.* **90.** you must thinck: *B.* **98.** that worke
forward: *I, II.* **106.** delight: *B, I, II.* **109.** exit: *omitted in III; M,
however, has* ext *here.* **110.** Magick glasse: *I, II*; glasse now: *B.* **112.** his
eyes: *I, II.* **113.** I'me confident: *B; no stage-direction in III.* **114.** *M has*
Enter agen *here.* **114–115.** *line-arrangement in T:* the Mirror/blest
mee...Habit. **116.** did not you: *B.* **117.** Not a foote (Sir): *I, II.*

page 98

122. Pawne, saw you mine: *I, II. Part of the speech-heading has crept into
the text.* **127–130.** *omitted in M.* **127.** delitious Beuties: *L.* **128.** to
you, modest payre: *B.* **132.** irrecoverable: *III.* **133–136.** *omitted in M.*
134. Chance, or Separation: *III.* **135.** *omitted in B.* **137–138.** *line-
arrangement in T:* reason/then, that.... **151.** grieves at this: *I, II.* **154.**
cannot be married: *III.* **157.** *omitted in M.* **158.** Sure you maye: *I, II.*

page 99

161. *omitted in M.* **169.** Ceremonies: *I, II.* **170.** see it done: *I, II.*
171. cozen 'em: *L, M.* **172.** exeunt: *omitted in B.*

IV. ii.

Headed: Scena Secunda: *L, M, III. Stage-direction:* The Bl. Knight,
& his Pawne: Then ye Fat Bishop: Then the Black-King: *M.* **1.** *speech-
heading omitted in T;* black Bishop: *T.* **2.** thy absolution: *I, II.* **4.**
pounds: *I, II, III.* **5.** live-of-life: *M.* **6.** gentle: *I, II.* **7.** my bum:
I, II. **9.** how now? quality: *I, II.* **10.** the paultrest foole: *I, II.* **12.**
without credit: *I, II.* **15.** I: *omitted in M.* **16–18.** *omitted in M.* **17.**
thinck it: *B.* **21–23.** *omitted in M.* **21.** Nay, an: *I, II.*

page 100

22. poore-pocht-soft reare: *I, II*; poore pouch'd: *III.* **26.** *omitted in III.*
28. to the masculine: *I, II.* **31.** *omitted in I, II.* **32–42.** *omitted in M.*
35. as lightly: *I, II.* **36.** strange stories: *I, II.* **37.** seducements: *I,
II.* **38.** heartily: *I, II.* **40.** I never feele a Tempest, a Leaffe-wind
stirring: *L.* **42.** huffs: *omitted in B.* **46.** money Matrons: *I, II.* **47.**
too: *omitted in all the other texts.* **50.** beedes, needles: *I, II.* **53.** Tobacco-
roles: *I, II.* **55.** turned: *III.*

page 101

59. I pray: *M.* **62.** fortifications: *I, II.* **64.** and learnd: *III.* **66.** proper'st: *omitted in I, II.* **68.** of each shippe, the brasse: *I, II.* **72.** best
Inhabitants: *III.* **78.** into the phisick: *I*; into physick: *II.* **81.** our black
House: *I, II.* **85.** penitentia: *B.* **87–88.** *line-arrangement in T:* this
halfe/hower, and.... **90.** Pawne: *omitted in III;* as I am: *I, II.* **94.** *B
has* killing *seven times, M three times, and L:* killing, killing, killing *etc.*

A Game at Chesse

96. Turne ore the sheete, you shall: *I, II;* and you shall: *III.* **100.**
Masse: *omitted in III.* **102.** or Daughter: *I, II.* **102–103.** thirteene pound:
L, M; and three pence: *I, II.* **104.** too: *omitted in M.* **111.** Sinnes:
III. **115.** (Sir): *omitted in I, II.* **117.** are too antient: *B.* **118.** as a
gratitud: *I, II.* **119.** thousands: *I, II.* **120.** Sir: *omitted in L.* **126.**
pounds: *I, II, III.*

131. that fact: *I, II.* **140.** my State: *III.* **141.** *omitted in T.* **142.**
speech-heading omitted in T. **143.** heart of game: *I, II.* **144.** Games
ouer: *B.* **147.** Surprizall (Sir): *B, III*; And for: *I, II.* **148.** in that:
I, II. **151.** *L has* ex^t *at the end of this line.* **152.** snatch'd: *III*; at next
bout: *L, M, I, II, III.* **153.** Game stands: *I, II.*

IV. iii.

Headed: Scena tertia: *L, M, III.* Recorder./Dumb shew./Enter
Blacke...: *I, II*; dumbe}showe} Recorders/Enter Bl....: *B*; Enter as in
a dumbe shew: *III*; A Domb/showe} The Bl:...: *L, M.* Pawne with
a light: *B, I, II*; with a Taper: *M, III*; (wth a Tapo^r in her hand): *L*;
conducting white Qs. Pawne to a chamber, and fetching in the Bl:
Bishops Pawne, conuayes him to another, putts out the light and
followes: *B, I, II, III; B adds* him; and Conducts ye wh. Queenes-
Pawne (in her Night Attire) into one Chamber; And Then Convaies
ye Bl. B^ps Pawne (in his Night habit) into an other Chamber, So puts
out ye Light, & followes him: *L; M agrees with L, except that it omits the
two* ands *and* (in his Night habit).

IV. iv.

Headed: Scena Quarta: *L, M, III.* The White-Knight, & Wh. Duke,
Y^en ye Bl. Knight: Then Y^e white-Queene: ye Fat Bishop: ye white
Bishop: & ye White King: *M.* **1.** Noble Knight: *T, B, I, II.*

3. cause and cunning: *I, II.* **6.** on: *omitted in I, II.* **8.** Triumphs:
I, II. **11.** in this: *B*; in his: *I, II.* **12.** buize: *T.* **13.** would see: *I, II.*
14. *no stage-direction in T, B.* **15.** in yonder perfidious: *B.* **19.** *in III all the
speeches of the Black Knight are prefixed with* B. K. *or* Bl. K., *and nearly all
of the White Knight with* W. K. *throughout this scene.* **20.** the House: *I, II.*
22–23. *line arrangement in T:* youre con-/fidence? I.... **22.** confidences:
B. **28.** taunted: *I, II.* **32–34.** and become...Tomboye: *omitted in M.
Between* **32** *and* **33** *III inserts the line,* (For your sake, and th' expulsion of
sad thoughts). **33.** of a great: *I, II*; State-Sir: *III.* **34.** yeare: *I, II.*
38. would stride: *I, II.*

40. of followers: *B.* **45.** To please you, to any shape: *I, II.* **50.** *T omits
the rest of the scene, and has* Finit Actus Quartus *after this line. The*

remaining 69 *lines are supplied from B.* **58.** *stage-direction omitted in B;* *supplied from L.* **62.** miserable: *I, II.* **63.** Tis in vaine: *I, II.* **64.** I *altered to* wee: *B.* **66.** *omitted in M, which completes* l. 65 *by adding to it:* there is no remedie. **66.** no deliverer: *L, I, II*; no deliver: *III.*

page 106

75. Bishop all this while that: *I, II.* **78.** of game: *B.* **84.** Be no longer mine: *I, II.* **88–91.** *omitted in M.* **94.** that workes: *I, II.* **95–98.** the properst...aduanced worke: *omitted in M.* **96.** in casting: *I, II.* **101.** the bag: *I, II.* **110–115.** *omitted in M.* **110.** you never were: *III.*

page 107

116. Goe (Reverend of men): *L, M, III.*

V. i.

Headed: Incipit Quintus et Ultimus: *B, I, II*; Actus Quintus, scena prima: *L, M, III. Stage-direction:* Lowe Musique: *B, but omitted in L, I, II, III*; Enter the Blacke Knight, in his Litter, as passing in hast over the Stage: *B, I, II*; Enter Blacke Knight and the Blacke Bishops Pawne above: *III*; Enter yᵉ Black-Knight (in his Littoʳ) and yᵉ Black-Bs Pawne (above): *L*; The Black-Knight (in his Litter) & yᵉ Bl: Bᵖˢ Pawne above: Then yᵉ Black-house (meeting the white Knight, and white Duke: *M.* **1.** *omitted in L, M.* **3.** Placed: *B*; Planted for his consecration: *I, II.* **5–6.** *line-arrangement in T:* Bishop Tum-/brell is snapt.... **6.** is snap: *B, I, II.* **9.** Away, away, make haste: *I, II, III.* Enter B. Ki. Q. D. & B. Kt. with Pawnes meeting the W. Kt. and Duke: the blacke Bishops pawne from above entertaines them with this Lattin Oration: *I, II*; hoboyes agen: Enter Bl. K. Q. Duke wᵗʰ Pawnes, meeting the white knight & duke the Bl: Bˢ Pawne aboue entertaining them wᵗʰ this Lattin oration: *B*; Enter Bl. K. Q. D. K. and Wh. Kni. and D.: *III*; Enter Black House, meeting yᵉ White-Kᵗ & Duke: *L.* **10–20.** the Oration *is printed as verse in I, II, III; the line-arrangement in all three is exactly the same.* **14.** acces- accessum: *T*; access- *is the last word of one page, and* accessum *the first word of the next.*

page 108

18. Affectibur: *T.* **24–33.** *omitted in T; these lines are supplied from B.* **25–33.** *omitted in M.* **27.** fixed on: *III.* **40.** the erroneous rellish: *omitted in III; in B, L, M, I, II these words are assigned to the White Duke.* Musique An alter discouered and statues standing on each side: *B*; Musicke: An altar is discovered with Tapers and Images standing on each side: *I, II*;...and divers Images about it: *III*; Musick an Altar discouered wᵗʰ Tapers on it: and diuers Images about it: *L; M agrees with L, except that it omits* diuers. **48.** *stage-direction omitted in T, B; but it is found in all the other texts, including M.*

page 109

51–52. *omitted in T.* **53.** *T erroneously gives this speech to* Wh. K.

A Game at Chesse

V. ii.

Headed: Scena Secunda: *L, M, III. Stage-direction:* Enter Wh:
Queenes Pawne and Bl. Bishops Pawne (in his reuerend habit)
meeting her: *B*; Enter White Q. p. and the Blacke B. p. the Jesuit in
his reverend habit meeting them: *I, II*; Enter severally Wh. Q s. p. and
Bl. Bishops Pawne in his reuerend habit: *III*; Enter ye white Queenes-
Pawne & ye Black-Bishops Pawne: *L*; The white Queenes Pawne &
Black-Bishop's Pawne Then ye Black Queenes-Pawne: Then ye white
Bishop's Pawne & ye Bl Knights Pawne: *M. In B this stage-direction
is the last of the portion of the play in the scribe's handwriting; from here to the
end the MS. is in Middleton's writing.* **1.** triall of my dutie now: *L, M, I,
II, III.* **2.** most modest: *III.* **5.** traytor to Holinesse: *omitted in T, B.*
7. How ill h'as us'd?: *I, II*; how ill 'hath usd me: *L, M, III.* **12.** *omitted
in M.* **13.** Bl. Qs. p.: *T*; Reuerend Respect: *M.* **16.** If I might counsell, you should never speake: *I, II, III*; you neuer should: *B.* **17.** un-
chastity: *I, II.* **18.** you will not: *I, II.* **20.** you'de count it strange: *B*;
to see a deuill: *L, M, I, II, III.* **26.** divilish part: *I, II.* **27.** as you
should, and: *I, II.*

page 110

30–36. *omitted in M.* **31.** they must have cunning judgments: *L, I,
II*; Judgement: *III.* **33.** mighty Auditory: *I, II.* **36.** the Game: *I, II.*
39. time (youths fortune): *I, II.* **42.** wch is: *B*; plauge: *T, B.* **46.** you
love: *I, II.* **51.** Strange of all men: *B, L, M, I, II, III*; should first light:
B, L, M, III. **53.** the business (sir); *I, II*; that Busynes (Sir): *L, M,
III.* **57.** you tyde once: *I, II*; that sacred: *M.* **58.** solliciting: *L, M, III.*
64. the Game: *I, II.*

page 111

69. Cunning: *I, II.* **76–77.** *line-arrangement in T:* chayre/in hell and
sitt.... **79.** sufferd: *M.* **79–80.** *line-arrangement in T:* to/bee lead, last
night.... **81.** Bl. Qs. P. within: *L, M; I, II, III have* Within *in the right
hand margin opposite this, and the other speeches of Bl. Qs. p. till her entrance;
L has* Bl. Qs. p. within *at the head of these other speeches, and M merely*
within. **84.** You may go now: *M.* **85.** This a: *T*; strange game
indeed: *I, II.* **87.** What the devil: *III.* **90.** Why: *omitted in I, II*; made
promise: *L, M, I, II, III.* **91.** after thanksgiuing: *T.* **92–94.** yes...not
to thee: *omitted in M.* **93.** Mischiefe confound: *I, II.* **94.** and you did
prepare youre selfe: *B.* **97.** slid, tis a bawdy Pawne: *B*; This is a bawdy
Pawne: *L, M, III*; This is some bawdy P.: *I, II.* **98.** What me your
bedfellow: *I, II.*

page 112

104. fild the place: *I, II.* **106–107.** praye looke...take it: *omitted in M.*
106. looke uppon mee (Sir): *III.* **107.** tis no longer: *L, I, II, III*;
longer (Sir): *M.* **110.** you purst: *I, II.* **114.** eares swell: *I. II.* **115.**
omitted in M. **124.** I cannot: *I, II.* **129.** hold bloudie Villayne: *B*;

Textual Notes

Oh bloody villain: *I, II*; How now blacke Villaine: *L, M, III*. **129–131**. *line-arrangement in T:* hold...heape a/murder on...time that/thou wert taken. **130**. fowle offence: *B, L, M, III*; offences: *I, II*; oh merciles Blood-hound: *omitted in T, B*. **132**. How? prevented: *L, M, III*. **133**. that partner: *L, M, I, II, III*.

page 113

V. iii.

Headed: Scena tertia: *L, M, III*. *Stage-direction:* The Black-House, & yᵉ white-Knight, & Duke: Then the white King, Queene, Bishop: *M*. **1**. You haue enricht: *all editions but T*; (Noble Sir): *III*. **5**. a thing wee seldome heare off: *B*. **6**. *omitted in B*. **12**. Ebusis: *I, II*. **14–16**. *omitted in M*. **17**. (Epicedian-like): *III*; crambd: *B*. **19–23**. *omitted in M*. **21–23**. *line-arrangement in T:* Of his...by th'/Inuentiõ, whose... followed. **25**. a Dinner: *I, II*. **30**. Wh. Kt.: *omitted in T, though this line is marked off as a separate speech.*

page 114

35. after sup: *I, II, III*. **42**. th' white house... espetially: *I, II*. **43**. wealthy fat Plebeians: *L, M*. **45–55**. *omitted in M*. **54**. stung to death: *I, II*; struck: *III*. **56**. (Sr): *omitted in I, II*. **57**. And cleare Abstinence: *I, II*. **59–60**. *omitted in M*. **61**. Bl. K.: *M*; talke of: *I, II*. **63–67**. *omitted in M*. **64**. Fognes of Fatnes: *T*. **66–67**. *Three lines in T:* Youre course...should trans/gresse...haue much/wrought mee to it. **67**. to it: *omitted in I, II, III*; if I should change: *B*. **68**. 'tis not: *I, II*.

page 115

72. *omitted in M*. **74–75**. *omitted in M*. **76**. Wh. Kt.: *omitted in T, but the speech is marked off as a separate one;* resolved in: *B, I, II*. **98**. her cheife Ouen: *T*.

page 116

107. full hopes: *L, I, II*. **108**. when we rise: *II*. **114**. but there's: *II*. **115**. another stands gaping for food: *I, II*. **119**. hanousnesse, that is: *I, II*. **122**. their pious: *III*. **123**. weake orizons: *L, I, II*. **126**. Pluto (whom: *I, II*. **127**. entombd there: *I, II*. **128**. *this speech lacks a prefix in T, though it is marked off as a separate speech.* **128–129**. *these two lines are transposed in L, M, I, II, III*. **130**. (Sir): *L, M, B, I, II*. **133**. so vilde: *L, M, I, II, III*. **138**. Claye, verily: *I, II*.

page 117

143. *this speech lacks a prefix in T, though it is marked off as a separate speech.* **144**. I, how? how: *L, I, II*. **158**. hiddest: *T*; the hidden'st poyson: *I, II*. **159**. smoothest Venome: *I, II*; Sʳ: *omitted in I, II*. **160–161**. *omitted in M*. **169**. 'Tis like a Jewell: *L, M, III*. **170–171**. *line-arrangement in T:* to the skillfull/Lapidarie, whose.... **174**. Now y'are a Brother to us: *assigned to Bl. D. in L, M, I, II*. **178**. *stage-direction in I, II only.*

135

page 118

180–181. *omitted in T.* **184.** Oh let my armes be blest: *I, II.* ·**186.** this faire Structure: *B, I, II.* **192.** I gave: *I, II.* **198.** *stage-direction from III; omitted in T, B;* the Bag open'd, the B. B. slides in it: *I, II;* The Bagge opens, and yᵉ Black Lost Pawnes appeere in it: *L;* The Bagg opens, & the Black-Side put into it: *M.* **201.** heades: *L.* **202.** Issues: *B.* **203–237.** *omitted in M.* **203.** Tis too apparent the Game's lost, King taken: *L, I, II.* **205–209.** *written as prose in T.* **205.** They had need give: *III.* **206.** has so ouerlayd mee: *B, L, I, II, III;* Fat Black Bishop: *L.* **207.** So squelcht and squeezde mee: *B, L, I, II, III.* **208.** if you looke: *B, I, II.*

page 119

214. too little: *I, II.* **215–216.** Order, I abhorre thee,/Thou't shew thy whorish front: *I, II;* Thou show: *L.* **218.** in the bag: *I, II.* **219.** Wh. K.: *omitted in T, but the speech is marked off as a separate one.* **221.** so: *omitted in L, III.* **223–224.** *III transposes the prefixes to these two speeches.* **228.** I'm sure to be the last man that creepes out: *I, II, III;* I am sure to be...: *L.* **230–231.** *found only in T, B.* **230.** the Politian: *B.*

page 120

EPILOGUE

7. in priuate lurke: *B, L, I, II, III.* **9.** bayle: *I.* **10.** Friends hands: *III.*

NOTES

Mr William Hammond seems to have belonged to a coterie of Middleton's civic patrons. Middleton's pious compilation, *The Marriage of the Old and New Testament* (1620), is dedicated to "the two Noble Examples of Friendship and Brotherhood, Mr. Richard Fishborne, and Mr. John Browne." Fishborne (a Mercer) and Browne (a Merchant-Tailor) were partners; and in Richard Fishborne's will Browne is named as the executor, while William Hammond was one of twenty friends who were each left five pounds for a mourning ring.

INDUCTION

8. the Ægiptian Grassehoppers: a very common term of abuse against the Jesuits. Cf. III, i, 90–98.

"For in the Catholique *Roman* Church, amongst all the disordered orders of swarming Locusts, which are almost innumerable, there is none but take their beginning from one supposed Saint or other."

T. Robinson: Anatomie of the English
Nunnerie at Lisbon (1622), p. 4.

"For their fulnesse of bread who knoweth not that they (like the caterpillers of *Egypt*) doe eate up the fat & best fruits of the land?" Gee's *New Shreds out of an Old Snare*, p. 13.

"Marry I thinke that when their blacke Synagogues at *Rome*, *Valladolid* and *Siuill* doe send forth their Locusts into *England*...."

Robinson's Anatomie, p. 19.

15–30. "The Bull of Loyola's canonisation was published by Urban VIII on August 6, 1623; his Beatification had been pronounced by Paul V in 1609. I have looked through the various accounts of Loyola in the *Acta Sanctorum* without finding anything to illustrate the passage in the text. Loyola's feast falls on July 31." Bullen.

24. Roch, Main, and petronell, Itch and ague—Curers.
"What particular office hath father *Ignatius?* or what part is there commonly assigned vnto him for the succour of men? for I make no doubt, but as God hath assigned to euery orher [*sic*] Saint the cure of some one disease or other, as to St. *Roch* the

plague, to St *Petronel* the feuer, to St. *Main* the itch, so St. *Ignatius* hath some certaine one vnto which hee is marvellously assisting."

State Mysteries of the Jesuites (1623), pp. 12–13.

28–29. Middleton is wrong here; the bisextile, or leap, year does not, of course, fall "once in three." It is called bisextile because in the Julian Calendar the sixth day before the Kalends of March was counted twice in leap year. *N.E.D.*

31–33. "*Jesuit.* .ᐧ.he [Loyola] had beene a debauched Souldier, & borne armes at *Pampelune* against the *French*, where hee was maymed, with an hurt that he receiued on both his knees, whereof hee halted euer after, but in such manner that it was hardly perceiued....

Novice. I feare that the Heretickes will draw some hard consequence from thence, and say that he is father of a Societie which halteth on both sides...."

State Mysteries of the Jesuites, p. 5.

ACT I, SCENE I

42–43. "Charitie hath her Armes full of children, & tenderbrested Compassion is still in one street or other doing good workes."   Dekker: *The Seven Deadly Sinnes of London* (1609), ed. H. F. B. Brett Smith, p. 51.

43–45. (he) "and his fellow-Iesuits...will cherish and nourish them, euen in their owne bosomes: such a burning zeale haue they towards them."   Robinson's *Anatomie*, p. 9.

46–47. The Black Queen's Pawn means that she is connected with the order founded by Mary Ward, on the model of that of the Jesuits. Sir Henry Wotton, in a letter to Lord Zouch on November 25, 1623, says:

"I have seen no novelty on the way fit to entertain your Lordship withal, save the English Jesuitrices at Liege, who, by St. Paul's leave, mean to have their share in Church service, as well as in needlework."

Life and Letters of Sir Henry Wotton, by L. Pearsall Smith (1907), vol. II, p. 283.

The first reference to these Jesuitesses in the pamphlet literature I have met with is not, however, until 1629, when the following passage occurs in *The English-Spanish Pilgrime* (p. 30):

"These three seuerall ranckes and Orders aforesaid are growne to a faction, about the Jesuitrices or wandering Nuns, some allowing, some disliking them utterly. This Order of

Nuns began some 12 yeeres since, by the meanes of Mistresse *Mary Ward*, and Mistresse *Twitty*, two *English* Gentlewomen, who obserue the *Ignatian* habit, and goe clad very like to the Iesuites, in this onely differing from other Nunnes: They walke abroad in the world, and preach the Gospell to their sex in *England* and elsewhere."

57. the Vniuersall Monarchie. The fear of the supposed Spanish aims for a world-empire is frequently expressed, and in v, iii, 91–102 the Black Knight is made to expound the extent of these ambitions. Many pamphlets deal with this subject, including *The Spaniards Perpetvall Designes to an Universall Monarchie* (1624). Two extracts from one of Middleton's sources give a succinct exposition of the idea:

Preamble to the message of the King of Spain:

"Whereas We had a hope by our Agents in *England* and Germanie to effect that great worke of the Westerne Empire; and likewise on the other side to surprize *Venice*, and so incircling *Europe* at one instant, & infolding it in our armes, to make the easier roade vpon the Turke in *Asia*, and at length reduce all the World to our Catholike command. And whereas to these holy ends We had secret and sure plots and proiects on foot in all those places, and good intelligence in all Courts..."   T. Scott: *Vox Populi*, pt 1 (1620), p. 31.

In another passage from the same tract Gondomar is made to say:

"My aimes haue euer beene to make profit of all, and to make my Master, Master of all.... And to this end I beheld the endeauours of our Kings of happie memorie, how they haue achieued Kingdomes and conquests by this policie, rather then by open hostilitie, and that without difference, as well from their *allies & kinsfolkes*, men of the *same Religion and profession*, such as were those of *Naples*, *France* and *Nauar*, though I doe not mention *Portugall* now vnited to us, nor *Sauoy* (that hardly slipt from us) as of an aduerse and hereticall Faith. Neither is this rule left off, as the present Kingdome of *France*, the State of *Venice*, the *Low-Countreys*, *Bohemia* (now all labouring for life vnder our plots) apparantly manifest." (p. 9.)

84–87. Cf. "A kiss now that will hang upon my lip
As sweet as morning dew upon a rose."
        Women Beware Women, III, i, 104–5.

86. A reminiscence of this line, by Milton, occurs in *Lycidas*, l. 26.

206–208 (cf. also II, i, 1–11 and 34–72):
"Their ghostly father hath composed sundry Treatises for
them of Obedience, wherein hee pronounceth no lesse then
damnation for the least scruple or hesitation in the performance
of their Superiours Commands. . . . Hauing made these books
of Obedience, he caused mee to write them out faire, omitting
in many places a Leafe, and in some two or three together,
which contained any false doctrine and vnallowable per-
swasions to draw them to obedience in vnlawful things; and
being finished in this sort, he bringeth them to Father *Newman*
to be signed with his approbation and testimonie, that there
was nothing in them repugnant to the Catholique faith; which
being done, hee then inserteth and soweth in the aforesaid
omitted Leaues, and so delivereth them to his daughters to
be practised, who take the approbation at the end of the booke
for a sufficient warrantie of all the doctrine therein contained.
And this is a principall furtherance of his sacriligeous lusts: for
I am verily perswaded that not one amongst them will (for
feare of being disobedient) refuse to come to his bed whenso-
euer he commands them: and that they doe so, I have mani-
festly seene and knowe."   Robinson's *Anatomie*, pp. 18–19.

235–237. "I could also adde, that in the gardens of Nun-
neries, was alwayes a tree or two of *Sauine*, which they say the
Nunnes vsed to drinke steeped in wine: now the property of
Sauine is to destroy any thing condensed in the wombe, and
so you may iudge of the cause."
        The Friers Chronicle (1622), E1v.–E2.

265–269. "*Novice.* I hearde an Hereticke not long since
make strange Glosses vpon this. Hee said vpon occasion of
Father *Bellarmins* reason that it was needful to haue new Orders,
because the feruor of the old by little and little grew cold, how
we held a good course that the like should not arriue vnto ours:
for besides the care we providently take that the great pot may
be alwayes boyling...we exercise the trade of incendiaries in
all places; and not contented with a thousand firings of houses,
made by our Institutor, we haue set all Christendome on
fire: neither is there any Kingdome, Commonwealth, City,
or Prouince, which we have not enflamed with warres and
seditions; and there said he, was our Father *Ignatius* most
properly compared to a Montigibel, the very tunnell of Hell."
        State Mysteries of the Jesuites, pp. 7–8.

278–287. (Gondomar is spoken of as) "having effected more by his wit and policy, then could haue beene wrought by the strength of many Armies."

> T. Scott: *The Second Part of Vox Populi* (1624), p. 58.

288–306. (Gondomar is supposed to be describing the release of Baldwin, a priest, from the Tower at his intercession in 1613.) "I solemnly went in person, attended with all my traine, and diuers other well-willers to fetch him out of the Tower where he was in durance. As soone as I came in his sight I behaued my selfe after so *lowly & humble a manner*, that our aduersaries stood amazed to behold the *reuerence we giue to our Ghostly fathers*. And this I did to *confound them* and their *contemptuous Clergie*, & to beget an extraordinarie opinion of *holynesse in the person* and *pietie in us*, & also to prouoke the English Catholikes to the like deuout obedience; and thereby at any time these Iesuites (whose authority was somwhat weakned since the Schisme betwixt them and the Secular Priests and the succeeding powder-plot) may worke them to our ends, as Masters their Seruants, Tutors their Schollers, Fathers their Children, Kings their Subjects."　　　　T. Scott: *Vox Populi*, pt 1, pp. 27–28.

325–340 (and also for II, i, 220–264). "The Iesuits were the first that did begin to swarme, and seeke further for a new hive, but they were sent away by course of expulsion, and open banishment out of the whole dominion, and that by a special decree.... There was an inuentory taken by an vnder Secretary and Commendatore, of the goods they left behinde them, and seased upon by the State, rather for curiosities sake, to know what they had gathered, then for any meaning that the State hath euer to bee accountable for any part thereof....

In which search haue bin discouered two memorable things: First a *Scrinio* (as they call it here) with partitions of their addresses to and from all parts, As *England, France, Spaine, Flaunders, Germany, Poland, Russia, &c.* with subdiuisions also of the Prouinces into Townes, as *London, Paris, Lions, Rome, &c.* And in this *Scrinio*, they had left, rather through vanity then hast, a great and incredible heape of the very ashes and tynder of their dispatches. The other was an artificial furnace, such as the *Italian* Goldsmiths doe vse for the dissoluing of gold and siluer which was brought into the Councell of Tenne, and hath bred much discourse; the best opinion being, that it was to

melt the chaines, rings, and iewels which they got from Gentlewomen, and so (*Mutata specie*) to put them away in Bullion."
*A Declaration of the Variance betweene the Pope and
the Segniory of Venice* (1606), pp. 32–35.

335. (Gondomar's advice to the Jesuits.) "Learne or devise
new and the most difficult Characters for writing Letters, with
all the slights and devises of privy conveyance."
The Second Part of Vox Populi, p. 56.

343–356. "Why quoth *Lewes de Valasco*, there should be nothing
so secretly carried amongst them, but we should know it.

The times (replyed *Gondomar*) are not now as heretofore, and
when I was in *England*; our best intelligencers, and the Catholiques are not in that grace that they haue beene: we haue had
in times past many friends, euen in the Parliament House."
The Second Part of Vox Populi, pp. 36–37.

"40th Proposition.

The *Jesuites* have learned one trick of *Machiavell* throughly
Practised by *Erasmus*, to be at composition with certaine *noble
men gentlemen* and others in Princes courts, to spread abroad
their workes... and there is no Prince in the world but hath
some *great Lord* or other about him that wilbe ready to speake
a good word for the *Jesuits....*

41st Proposition.

The no lesse consciencelesse than mercilesse *Jesuits* collect
great summes of money over all the Realme, & wherefore is all
this done? Because the greatest enterprises taken in hand by
them, are done more by *bribes* given to brokers, and great
promises made to them, that are sticklers for them; for the
later it hath beene long the function of the Religious *Fathers*
so to doe, to put men to great expectation of favour and advancement when their day shall come, & to ring every yeare
fresh Alarums of foreign preparation...."
The Downfall of the Jesuits (1612).

It should be noted, however, that the Jesuits and the
Spaniards were not the only ones who, through their "intelligencers," had access to "important secrets of state";
cf. Goodman's *Court of King James* (1839), vol. I, pp. 183–4
and n.

ACT II, SCENE I

1–11 and *34–72.* See note on I, i, 206–208.

73–80. "When any of the Priests knauerie was discouered, there were excuses enough ready to defend them; yea, when they were found kissing a woman; the answer was, You must suppose he did it to print a blessing on her lips."

The Friers Chronicle, f. Cɪv.

194. The marginal note to the passage quoted in the note on ɪ, i, 206–208 is:

They forget the old caveat, *Caute si non caste.*

220–264. See the note on ɪ, i, 325–340.

234–237. "If, about Bloomesbury or Holborne, thou meet a good smug fellow in a gold-laced suit...then take heed of a Jesuite." J. Gee: *Foote out of the Snare* (1624), p. 50.

Drury Lane was also a haunt of the Catholics; Bullen quotes from the speech of Mr Whitaker in the House of Commons, June 5, 1628: "In Drury Lane there are three families of Papists residing there for one of Protestants: insomuch that it may well be called little Rome."

ACT II, SCENE II

2–4. "He (de Dominis) was of a comely personage, tall stature, gray beard, grave countenance, fair language, fluent expression, somewhat abdominous, and corpulent in his body."

Fuller: *Church History of Britain* (1655), bk x, p. 100.

Compare this pen-portrait with the engraving on the title-page of the good quarto of the play and the portrait facing p. 71.

17–18 and *94–106.* Middleton has justifiably satirised the eagerness which de Dominis displayed in circulating his writings amongst his Protestant patrons. There are various references to this in the *Calendar of State Papers* (*Domestic*). On August 4, 1617, Archbishop Abbot announced that he had heard that the King had received the title and some leaves of the Archbishop of Spalato's book, while on the 17th of the same month de Dominis himself wrote to Sir Dudley Carleton, sending copies of his work for Prince Maurice and the States. A somewhat later letter, from Naunton to Buckingham (dated August 3, 1619), announces that the Archbishop of Spalato will wait on the King with his sixth book, *De Potestate Principum.* The book referred to in the text is probably *M. A. de Dominis...suae Profectionis Consilium exponit, Londini* (1616), in which he gives his reasons for coming to England.

35–38. "Preferment is quickly found out, and conferred upon him: as, the Deanrie of *Windsor* (though founded, not in a Cathedral, but Collegiate Church) one of the gentilest and entirest Dignities of the Land; the Mastership of the Hospital of the *Savoy*, with a good Parsonage at *West-Islely* in *Berk-shire*, being a Peculiar belonging to the Episcopal Jurisdiction of the Deane of *Windsor*. . . . Thus had he two Houses furnished above plenty, even unto magnificence, and might alternately exchange society, for privacy, at pleasure."

> Fuller's *Church History*, bk x, p. 94.

Fuller also tells how de Dominis, on hearing a false report of the death of the Archbishop of York, hastened to petition the King for the vacant see (p. 96). A letter from Thomas Locke to Sir Dudley Carleton (dated November 24, 1621) admirably illustrates the ambition and the avarice of the foreign prelate:

"The Bp: of Spalato sent to me againe to come to him, wch I would haue done wthout sending for, if I had knowne of his being in towne. And though I told him that yor Lp: intended to gratifie him according to yor promises, yet he grewe verie impatient; he said he perceiued that yor Lp: went about to mocke him, but he would not be so serued, the K should knowe it, And you had bin better peradventure to haue giuen 1000^{li}. I desiered him to haue a little patience, & not to Conceiue such a thought, I told him that yor Lp: did thincke yo^u might expect so much at his hands, And that I thought yo^u had bin as good a tenant to him as any other And that in this perticular you should be as thanckfull, in performing what you intended, as any other had bin, Then he said that Si^r Jo: Kidderminster had dealt better with him, And that he had neuer borrowed nor a farthing of yor Lp:. I asked him whether there could be no other services performed but in borrowing of money, not that he had receiued (he replied) vnlesse yo^u would yor words you had spoken to bring him hither, for wch yor Lp: receiued honor in that he was come into the land, yet that yo^u fayled in yor promise to help him to 200^{li} p añu⁹ from my Lo: of Cant. wch he did not now inioy accordinglie; I told him that peradventure my Lo: of Cant. did thincke him sufficientlie provided for otherwise, he said 300 nor 4 nor 500^{li} a yeare . . . were sufficient for him, he was a Prelate &c., And for the gratuitie that he was to receiue of yor Lp: it was verie smal for he protested he gaue a cleere 300^{li} that he might haue had, wth a greate deale of such like." *S.P. (Dom.)*, *James I*, vol. 123, no. 123.

42–46. "As for some turpitude of his (when he lived here, which was kept a while very covert) I had rather it should be buried still, than defile my pen, my selfe, and the world with the discoverie of it, except I should be inforced to it.... Yet I will indit him as guilty of these foure: An *arrogant Impostor*; an *irreligious Sycophant*; a *luxurious glutton*; a *perjured Apostate*, Pride being linkt with *Imposture*, Irreligion with *Slander*, Lechery with *Gluttony*, and *Periurie* with *Apostasie.*"

Newes from Rome, Spalato's Doome (1624).

47. "He improved the profit of his places to the utmost, and had a designe to question all his Predecessours Leases at the Savoy; and began to be very vexatious to his Tenants. Some of them repaired to Doctor *King*, Bishop of *London*; who, at their request, took *Spalato* to task, and gravely, as sharply reproved him: that, being a Forreigner, he would fall out with Natives, endevouring to put others here out of their peaceable Possessions, who himself had fled hither for his own refuge."

Fuller's *Church History*, bk x, p. 94.

48–50. "Amongst other of his ill qualities, he delighted in *ieering*, and would spare none who came in his way. One of his *sarcasmes* he unhappily bestowed on Count *Gondomar*, the *Spanish* Ambassador, telling him, That *three turns* at Tiburne *was the onely way to cure his Fistula.*"

Fuller's *Church History*, bk x, p. 95.

52. [On his arrival in England] "the KING consigned him to the Archbishop of *Canterbury*, for his present entertainment, till he might be accomodated to subsist of himself: and, as an earnest of His bounty, sent him to *Lambeth*, a faire *bason*, and *bolle of silver.*"

Fuller's *Church History*, bk x, p. 94.

"30 Decembris [1620]...A warrant to the Jewell house for 300 oz or thereabouts of faire guilt plate to be given by his Matie to the Archp. of Spallato in like sorte as the yeare before."

Pettyt MS. no. 515.7 (in the library of the Inner Temple) containing the Lord Chamberlain's Office Book, 1620–1621.

78. Baloom Ball: Nares, in his *Glossary*, says that the "baloon" was "a large inflated ball of strong leather, used in the game of the same appelation." He quotes a description of the game from a book called *Country Contents*:

"A strong and moveing sport in the open fields, with a great ball of double leather filled with wind, and driven to and fro with the strength of a man's arm, armed with a bracer of wood."

166–169. Taunts against the priests for not observing fasts in the spirit in which they should be observed are very common in the anti-Catholic pamphlets; in *The Friers Chronicle*, for instance, a whole section is devoted to the subject.

185–186. These lines probably contain a reference to a controversy that had centred around the pretensions of the priests to exorcise evil spirits, and certain subjects had given out that they were possessed with demons. The exposé of the case that attracted most attention was contained in *The Boy of Bilson: or a True Discovery of the Late Notorious Impostures of Certaine Romish Priests in their pretended Exorcisme* (1622), but there are many references to this and similar cases in the pamphlets, especially in Gee's *Foote out of the Snare* and in *The English-Spanish Pilgrime*.

194. For the doctrine of Equivocation, see the note on *Macbeth*, II, iii, 9 in the *New Variorum* edition.

240–241. The popular Protestant idea of the way in which cardinals' hats were granted seems to have been rather crude. Another example may be cited from *Vox Coeli* (1624), p. 39:

"*P. H.* Indeed, if *Gondomar* can effect this match, it is the direct way for him to be a *Grande* of *Spaine*, and to procure a red Hat for his Sonne or Nephew.

Q. A. Was the Duke of *Monteleone* so rewarded for his *French* matches?

Q. M. He is already a *Grande* of *Spaine*, and hath the promise of a Hat.

Q. A. Why then Count *Gondomar* neede not feare, for he hath as much policie as the Duke of *Monteleone*, though not so much ostentation."

271. Gondomar is said to have achieved his ends "with the quintessence of his *Castilian*, or rather *Galician* braine."
Vox Coeli, p. 45.

285–286. The pictures referred to here were actually by the artist Giulio Romano. They were a series of scandalous illustrations to some equally scandalous verses by Pietro Aretino. For the trouble which accrued to all concerned, even in the Italy of the opening years of the sixteenth century, see J. A. Symonds: *The Renaissance in Italy: Italian literature*, vol. II, p. 389.

146

ACT III, SCENE I

1–78. Middleton's source for these events was very probably *Newes from Rome: Spalato's Doome* (1624); chap. IV of that pamphlet shows "how this *Dalmatian* Mountebancke *M. Anthony*, came to be fully discovered by the practise of the *L. Gundamar*, Embassadour from the Kinge of Spaine":

[Gondomar] "comes to Spalato, and tells him, that though some unkindnesse had passed betweene them, yet at length hee would be his friend, and was sorie, considering his Learning and incomparable deserving, hee should live here in *England*, where hee assurede him hee was much maligned, and used but as a Stale, hereafter to publish store of books in his name. He said hee would undertake hee should be made a Cardinall upon his returne into his owne Countrey, where many his friends bemoaned him, and *Paul*, the then Pope, would thinke it a great happinesse to see him. For (saith hee) I can shew you a letter lately come to my hands from his *Holinesse*, who writes unto mee, desiring to be certified what is become of you, and if I speake with you, to signifie how much he desires your Good, and that hee will exceedingly further your preferment, if you shal come unto him; and so *Gundamar* drawes out of his pocket the pretended Letter from the Pope and bids him reade it; which containing many sugred promises of preferment, if *Spalato* should come to him to *Rome*: the Sun-shine thereof presently dazeled his eies, and the titular *Dalmatian* Bishop, who before like another *Leviathan* would drinke up *Iordan*, and overthrow the Popes Supremacie, now presently promiseth to joine forces with him: and told the L. *Gundamar* that if he meant well toward him, he would returne home to *Rome*. *Gundamar* all this while, like a craftie *Hiæna*, though he spake like a friend, devoured like a foe. . . . His plot was to bring him in disgrace here in England, and then to pack him over to Rome in a Cloake bag, where hee might live neere the fresh aire of the *Inquisition*." (pp. 22–24.)

A briefer, but similar, account is given in one of Chamberlaine's letters to Carleton (March 30, 1622):

"*Spalato* is this afternoon conuented at Lambeth before the Archbishop of caunterburie, the L. Keeper and divers other bishops, besides the L. President and secretarie Caluert so that we shall shortly see what becomes of him, I thinck his liuings be disposed of alreadie, the voice goes that the Spanish ambassador when he had brought him to his bent, told that now that he was unmasked and shewed himself what he was, he might take his choice whether to starue here or go ouer and be burnt, for he would haue no more to do wiᵗʰ him."

S.P. (Dom.), James I, vol. 128, no. 96.

Gardiner (*History of England,* vol. IV, p. 287 n.) doubts if Gondomar can have had anything to do with the departure of de Dominis from England, but Sir Henry Wotton, in one of his ambassadorial letters from Venice, reports otherwise (L. Pearsall Smith: *Life and Letters of Sir Henry Wotton,* vol. II, pp. 228–229). Writing to Calvert on March 6, 1622, he gives the substance of a secret audience accorded by the Pope to the Spanish Ambassador at Rome. The Pope agreed privately that a safe-conduct should be granted to the Archbishop of Spalato, but expressed his disapproval of the intention of the King of Spain to confer on him the bishopric of Salerno.

14. poore Alms Knights; i.e. the Poor Knights of Windsor.

54–55. "The recantation (a document of doubtful authenticity) was published in 1623, under the title—*Marcus Antonius de Dominis, Archiepisc. Spalaten, sui reditus ex Anglia consilium exponit, Romae.*" (Bullen.) An English translation was published at Douai.

88–91. Dyce and Bullen quote here a passage from Wilson's *Life and Reign of James I* (1653), p. 145:

"By his Artifices and Negotiations (having been time enough Ambassador in England to gain credit with the King) he [Gondomar] got Sir Robert Mansell to go into the Mediterranean sea, with a Fleet of Ships to fight against the Turks at Algier, who were grown too strong and formidable for the Spaniard (most of the King of Spain's Gallions attending the Indian Trade, as Convoys for his Treasures, which he wanted to supply his Armies) and he transported Ordnance and other Warlike Provisions to furnish the Spanish Arsenalls, even while the Armies of Spain were battering the English in the Palatinate."

The fleet in question left Plymouth in August, 1620.

Gardiner: *History of England,* vol. III, p. 374.

91–99. See also note to Induction, l. 8. " . . .an inlet to the romish Locuste, which like the Canker-worme may in an instant smite our Gourd, under whose shadow we sit safe."

Alured's "honest letter" from MS. Dd. III, 84, U.L.C.

148

101–103. "And that they may do this the more boldly & securely, I haue somwhat dasht the authoritie of their *High Commission*: vpon which whereas there are diuerse Purseuants (men of the worst kind and condition, resembling our Flies and Familiars, attending vpon the Inquisition) whose office and imployment it is to disturbe the Catholikes, search their houses for Priests, Holy vestments, Books, Beades, Crucifixes, and the like religious appurtenances, I haue caused the execution of their office to be slackned. . . . And yet when these Purseuants had greatest authoritie *a small bribe in the Country* would blinde their eyes, or *a little greater at Court* or in the Exchequer, frustrate & crosse all their actions."

Vox Populi, pt I, p. 28.

103–104. "The Romane Catholiks of England haue reason to beleeue *Gondomar*; sith King IAMES loues him so well, as hee esteemes his speeches Oracles and Scripture; and who with the quintessence of his *Castillian*, or rather *Galician* braine hath now brought matters to this passe, that no sincere aduise, honest Letter, Religious Sermon, or true picture can point at the King of *Spaine*, but they are called in; and their Authours imprisoned (insted of rewarded) though neuer so true and loyall Subiects."   *Vox Coeli*, p. 45.

In the very letter to Carleton in which he relates the performance of *A Game at Chesse* (see Appendix A), Nethersole announces the imprisonment of the author of the pamphlet from which this extract is taken: "Mr. Reynolds, Viscount Fielding's tutor, is imprisoned for writing two pamphlets, Vox Coeli and Votiva Anglia, with which the King is much displeased." Both *Vox Coeli* and *The Second Part of Vox Populi* give a list of preachers punished for their outspokenness through Gondomar's influence. They include Alured (for his "honest letter" to Buckingham), Dr Everard, Whiting, and Clayton (for a sermon called *The Spanish Ewe*).

The *Directions concerning Preachers* (issued in 1622) are printed in full by Rushworth: *Historical Collections*, vol. I, pp. 64–65. They ordered "that no Preacher . . . shall presume . . . to declare, limit, or bound out . . . the Power, Prerogative, and Jurisdiction, Authority, or Duty of Sovereign Princes, or otherwise meddle with matters of State . . . or fall into bitter Invectives, and indecent railing Speeches against the Persons of either *Papists* or Puritans."

106–107. The reference here is to an engraving by the Rev. Samuel Ward, of Ipswich, called *1588 Deo Trin-uni Britanniæ*, which was suppressed. For a note on Ward, see *N. & Q.* (4th series), vol. XI, p. 386.

141. "For the generall it is well knowne that many priests could scarce read Latin, much lesse understand it and knew not their Masse and Mattens but by the great letters."

The Friers Chronicle, ff. F30–F4,

301–310. It is interesting to compare with these lines a passage from Massinger's *Bondman*, which, as Gardiner points out in his paper on *The Political Element in Massinger's Plays* (*Transactions of the New Shak. Soc.* (1875–6), pp. 317–318), also refers to Middlesex:

"those
Who, rising from base arts and sordid thrift,
Are eminent for their wealth, not for their wisdom;
Which is the reason that to hold a place
In council, which was once esteemed an honour,
And a reward for virtue, hath quite lost
Lustre and reputation, and is made
A mercenary purchase."   (Act. I, sc. iii.)

ACT III, SCENE III

This scene makes use of a device that had already been employed on the stage in Rowley's play, *A Shoo-maker a Gentleman,* and possibly this conjuring with mirrors was commoner on the stage than has been suspected. It is quite clear, from the stage-direction at l. 56: "Enter the Jesuite... presents himself *before* the mirror," and from the Black Queen's Pawn's injunction to her victim that she must "observe the right use...

Not looking back, or questioning the Specter"

(III, i, 395),

that the Black Bishop's Pawn came on to the stage behind the White Queen's Pawn and stood so that she could see him reflected in the mirror. The passage in Rowley's play is as follows:

"*Leodice.* ... I have some skill in Magicke, what would you
    give
To see her amply personated in a glasse,
That must be your wife?

 Crispinus. I would venture a chiding to stay thus long: but
  what may this mean?
 Leo. I could by Metroscopie read thy fate
Here in thy fore-head: by Chyromancie find it
In thy Palme, but these are petty Arts, no Ile shew thee
By speculatory magick, her face in this glasse;
Kneele sir, for't must be done with reverence
I telle you: now tell me what thou seest?
 Cris. I see a shadow Madam.
 Leo. 'Tis but a shadow, hold up thy right hand and looke
Agen, what seest thou now? any substance yet?
 Cris. I know not Madam, I am inchaunted with your Magick.
 Leo. How lik'st her now, has she a good face?
 Cris. Tis very well made Madam.
 Leo. Who does she resemble?
 Cris. Your selfe, I thinke Lady.
 Leo. I, shees very like me.
 Cris. I would she were not.
 Leo. Why wouldst not have her like me?
 Cris. Because no like's the same.
 Leo. 'Tis too long to dally, away with shadowes,
And imbrace the substance, in troth I love thee."
     A Shoo-maker a Gentleman, II, iii, 148–171.

ACT IV, SCENE I

1–12. "Their penury is turned into plenty; their chastity
becomes charity for the relieving of collapsed ladies wants:
their friers coat is a gold-laced suit, to hide their juggling
knavery, and keepe them unknowne, when they are drunke
in good company."

"If, about Bloomesbury or Holborne, thou meet a good
smug fellow in a gold-laced suit, a cloke lined thorow with velvet,
one that hath gold rings on his fingers, a watch in his pocket,
which he will valew above 20 pounds, a very broad-laced band,
a stiletto by his side, a man at his heeles, willing (upon small
acquaintance) to intrude into thy company . . . then take heed
of a Jesuite."

"The Jesuits have the superlative cognizance whereby they
know one another; and that is, as I observed from this time,
a gold hat-band studded with letters or characters."

     Gee's *Foote out of the Snare,* pp. 50 and 69.

154–161. [Chap. III. Cases in which Equivocation is allowed.]

"*9. If a man be forced to promise marriage to a woman, whom otherwise he is not bound to marrie* (the meaning is, if he be vrged and pressed by a Iudge against reason, to make that promise) *he may sweare, that hee will marry her*, though hee meane it not, *understanding within himselfe, If I be bound to doe so, or, if afterward I shall like of it.*"

Henry Mason, *New Art of Lying* (1624), p. 51.

ACT IV, SCENE II

27–31. "Lastly, I left behind me such an Instrument *composed artificially of a Secular vnderstanding and a religious profession*, as he is euerie way adapted to scrue himselfe into the closet of the heart, and to worke vpon feminine leuitie, who in that Countrey haue masculine Spirits to command and pursue their plots vnto death." *Vox Populi*, p. 20.

43–47. "Sir *Robert Cotton* a great Antiquary, I heare, much complaineth of me, that from his friends and acquaintance onely I got into my purse the summe at the least of ten thousand pounds, I deny it not and true it is that I borrowed of the good old Lady *W.* of the Parish in *St. Martins* in the Fields 300 pounds, or thereabouts, promising her repayment (whereof I will not faile) so soone as *Donna Maria*, the *Infanta*, should arrive in *England*, and for the vse hereof, I promised to make her mother of the maydes, perswading her, it was not fit so graue and good a Lady as her selfe should lye obscured in priuate, but rather attend vpon my young Mistresse, the brauest and most hopefull Princesse of the World: vpon these hopes she turned Catholique; and since then I neuer saw her." *The Second Part of Vox Populi*, p. 11.

"I sold moreouer the place of Groomesse of her highness Stoole to six seuerall English Ladyes, who were eager of it, only because they might take place before their fellowes." *The Second Part of Vox Populi*, p. 11.

47–53. "If you would at any time convey over any Silver or Gold, the Searcher commonly may be couzoned, if you send it over in Pasties baked, provided that you haue some of flesh onely to eate or giue away, as a cullor for the rest. For the venting of hallowed Oile, Beades, *Agnus-Deies*, Meddalles, Pardons, Crucifixes, &c. You may doe it by some one poore yet Trustie Catholique or two, to goe vp and downe the Countrie in the habit and nature of Pedlers: this also is a good way to hold intelligence with friends in many places. I have knowne some vnder the cullour of selling *Tobacco*, haue carried Letters handsomly, privily in the balls or roules."

The Second Part of Vox Populi, pp. 56–57.

54–59. "Nothing lesse (quoth *Gondomar*) for I am perswaded though many will colourably depart though they returne againe shortly by new ports and new names more will remaine behind, (and since neuer likely againe to haue such an opportunity of professing themselues openly and exercising their functions, which they could do in a friends Chamber, and many times in the common Innes) for the better avoyding suspition, and concealing themselues, some will turne Schoolemaisters in priuate mens houses, as there are many in *England*, some Gentlemen vshers vnto Collapsed Ladies, as some such there are in *Drury*-lane: the L. T. in *Yorkeshire* hath one followes her in that nature; the L. S. not farre from my old house in *Holborne* in *London*; the L. M. neere unto *Stratford-bow*: Some *Falconers* whereof I know two, the one in *Sussex*, the other in high *Suffolke*, only one I was acquainted withall, who was the Keeper of a Parke, and a good Huntsman, and of whom I haue had many a good peece of Venison, if he be living, I know another Priest, who hauing liued with an ancient Lady of great estate, and of good credit, by reason he was enuironed with a pestilent crew of Puritanes on every side, and the better to colour his absence from the Church, learned the arte of Cookery, and is growne so expert therein, within a short space, that hee is able to dresse a Dinner with such arte, and good meate, . . . and his manner is, when hee hath layed his meate to the fire, to goe and say Masse."

The Second Part of Vox Populi, pp. 29–30.

60–69. "During the time of my abode in *England* and whilst I lay in *London*, I got partly by the means of well-affected friends and partly by mine own experience (for in sommer time under the colour of taking the ayre, I would take view of the countrey) I had perfect knowledge of the state of the whole Land: for there was no Fortification, Hauen, Creeke, or Landing-place about the Coast of *England*, but I got a platforme and draught thereof, I learned the depth of all their Channels, I was acquainted with all Sands, Shelves, Rocks, Rivers that might impeach or make for inuasion. I had perpetually in a Role the names of all the Ships of King *Iames* his Navy Royall, I knewe to a haire of what burthen euery ship was, what

153

Ordinance she carried, what number of Saylors, who were the Captaines, for what places they were bound."
The Second Part of Vox Populi, p. 15.

70–75. "I was no lesse diligent for the discouery of the Inland, then for the Shores and Sea-coasts: For there was neuer a Shire in *England*, but I better knew the estate, power and quality thereof then the Inhabitants, euen the best of them themselves did. I could in particular relate the nature of the soyle, what power of men and horse they were able to raise, who were the chiefe and of most ability and credit in the Countrey, who the most antient Gentlemen, what they were worth in their reuennues and estates, how they stood affected in Religion, who were Puritanes, and who Catholiques, and among Catholiques who stood for us, and who (for such there were) were indifferent or against vs."
The Second Part of Vox Populi, pp. 16–17.

85–115. Middleton was probably acquainted with one of the forged Protestant versions of the *Taxæ*, such as the *Taxe des Parties Casuelles de la Boutique du Pape, en Latin & en François....* Par A. D[u] P[inet] A Lyon 1564. The question of the authenticity of the different versions is discussed at length by Dr Gibbings in his Introduction to *The Taxes of the Apostolic Penitentiary* (Dublin, 1872). All the sins referred to in this passage are mentioned in du Pinet's book (pp. 57–81); there is also a section "De Mutilatione" (p. 56), but what sort of mutilation is not specified. The section on homicides of different kinds is certainly the largest in the book, and occupies pp. 57–72. It is Middleton, however, and not the Fat Bishop, who has "altered many of the sums."

101–103. "Absolutio pro eo, qui Matrem, Sororem, aut aliam consanguineam, vel affinem suam, aut Commatrem, carnaliter cognovit...G.v."
Gibbings: *The Taxes of the Apostolic Penitentiary*, p. 3.

105–107. Cf. Bandello: *Novelle*, pt II, nov. 35, and the *Heptameron*, nov. 30. Dunlop's *History of Fiction* has a long note on these tales (vol. II, pp. 219–224). It seems clear from what is said there that this is an old piece of folk-lore although Bandello states that his story is founded on fact. Dunlop quotes an old French rime that is said to have been an epitaph on a tomb-stone:

Cy-gist la fille, cy-gist le père,
Cy-gist la soeur, cy-gist le frère,
Cy-gist la femme, cy-gist le mary,
Et si n'y a que deux corps icy.

122–128. "It is well known they [the English nuns] have ten thousand pounds at vse in the Towne-house of *Antwerpe*.... Likewise when they remained in *France*, they had the custodie of no small summe of money, which was sent to them to keepe for Doctor *Lopez*, the Portuguese, as his reward for poysoning our late Queene *Elizabeth* of famous memorie, which after that Traitor (hauing missed of his intent) was executed, was remitted vnto them as almes, as the Register-booke of their house (from whence I had it), shameth not to make mention."
Robinson's *Anatomie*, pp. 9–10.

ACT IV, SCENE IV

35–42. [part of a discussion on the credibility of miracles] "Nor that a young married wife shall haue a child the same yeare if she can stride ouer at once Saint *Rombauts* breeches at *Mechlin*." *The Second Part of Vox Populi*, p. 38.

ACT V, SCENE I

1–24. "All the world wishes him (Prince Charles) here again, for the Spanish delayes are like to weare out his patience as well as ours... the Pope hath written to him already... and our fugitive countrimen of the seminaries there haue bin nibling at him too wth orations, whereof one that I saw is not worth the looking after either for matter or phrase."
Chamberlain to Carleton, June 28, 1623.
S.P. (Dom.), James I, vol. 147, no. 80.

41–52. "Are not yet men liuing, that can remember the knauerie of Priests to make the Roodes and Images of the Churches in *England* in the dayes of Queene *Mary*, to goggle with their eyes, and shake their hands: yea, with Wiers to bend the whole body, and many times to speake as they doe in Puppet playes, and all to get money, and deceiue the ignorant people?" *The Friers Chronicle*, f. B3v.

"Let anti-masques not be long; they have been commonly of fools, satyrs,...statues moving, and the like."
Bacon: *Of Masques and Triumphs.*

ACT V, SCENE II

101–112. "But now if any man demand, how and by what meanes they are brought thither; and by whom they are maintained: let him know, that there lurketh in *England* an arch-Traytour, one *Henry Flood*, a Jesuit, who is the chiefe Agent for the transporting of Nunnes, both to *Bruxels, Greueling, Lisbon,* or any other place; and whither he pleaseth to send them, thither they must goe. If they haue no portion, and perhaps some little honestie, they are not for the Iesuits tooth, *Aquila non capit Muscas,* they must packe to *Greueling,* to the poore bare-footed *Clares.* If they haue a small portion, that likes not the Iebusite neither: a pound of butter is nothing amongst a cure of hungry Hounds; *nec vacat exiguis rebus adesse Joui;* then away they trudge to *Lisbon,* where they are allowed daily fiue crownes, and their bread, and many a good almes beside is often bestowed vpon them. But if they haue a good round summe for their dowrie, *ab Inferno nulla est redemptio,* there is no plucking them out of the Iesuits Iawes; they are stamped for *Bruxels,* and thither must they goe; where *Fitz-herbert* and his fellow Iesuits will quickly dispossesse them of all worldly cares and vanities, and (like subtill Alchymists) refine them out of their siluer and golden drosse, into a more sublime estate and condition. . . ."

Robinson's *Anatomie,* pp. 8–9.

116–118. "A certaine Catholick collapsed lady. . . about some two or three years since, departed from her husband yet living, and went over to Bruxels, and was admitted into the order of nunnery, I meane a nunne at large, one of the un-cloystered sisters in the order of St. Clare and there she remained a while till there appeared in her some passion incompatible with nunship. Shee came over into England a companion with a religious Jesuit, since of great note, F.D., and remaining afterwards an inlarged nun in London, was, as it seemeth, more visibly taken with a disease befalling that sexe called *flatus uterinus:* and thereupon that this matter might be carried the more cleanly, it was given out, that she was possessed with an evill Spirit, which did make her belly swell like a woman with child."

Gee's *Foote out of the Snare:*
Somers' Tracts, ed. Scott, vol. III, p. 75.

"In a Village neere *Corgnac,* called *Cherues,* a Maid was got with child by her owne Brother, which she discouered to a Priest, and he perswaded the people *Impregnatam a spiritu.*"

The Friers Chronicle, f. D ɪ v.

ACT V, SCENE III

7–55. Dyce and Bullen both point out that there are a number of mistakes in this passage: *Eleusis* for *Ebusus* in l. 12, and *Sergius Crata* for *Sergius Orata* in l. 18, while in l. 34 Didius Julianus has been confused with Julian the Apostate. It is doubtful, however, if these mistakes are Middleton's—for, in the one instance, *Sergius Orata* would spoil the metre. It is much more probable that he was merely versifying the words of some book at his elbow, as he so often does in the course of the play, and the mistakes are those of his original. *Eleusis* and *Crata* could easily be printers' errors, and the confusion between the two Julians could be attributed to the author, who may perhaps have been the "new Laureat" referred to by Nashe in the following passage:

"The Romain Emperours that succeeded *Augustus* were exceedingly given to this horrible vice [gluttony], whereof some of them would feed on nothing but the tongues of Pheasants and Nightingales: other would spend as much at one banquet, as a kings revenues came to in a yeare; whose excesse I would decypher at large, but that a new Laureat hath sau'd me the labor."

Pierce Peniles (Works of Thomas Nashe,
ed. McKerrow, vol. ɪ, p. 199).

31–75. "The English report since their comming home, they neuer came unto a baser Country in their liues, where they could get meate neither for themselues or their horses, nor saw so much as one handfull of grasse in two hundred miles riding, and if they dined at one place, they were faine to go 30 or 40 miles ere they could get anything to their supper and then perhaps a peece of leane Kid, or Cabrito, a Tripe, Tone's or such like, indeede I remember when the Prince lay at *Madrid,* we were faine to send seauenteene miles off for a Calfe, for his highnesse Dyet, as for Mutton we may kill none without especiall Licence from the King, for fish our Riuers affoord none, and we being most temperate our selues, how should our dyet agree with their stomackes, who are accounted the greatest feeders of the World."

157

The marginal note to this passage is: *He that surfets at a Spaniards Table, trust me I will pay for his physicke.*
The Second Part of Vox Populi, pp. 21–22.

66–178. Cf. *Macbeth*, iv, iii, 1–139.

159. In *Vox Populi* (p. 13) Duke Pastrana is made to say: "I haue some cause to doubt, *since they* [the English] *can dissemble as well as we*, that they haue their aymes vnderhand, as we haue, and entend the match as little as we doe," but Gondomar replies that they "haue no patience to temporize and dissemble in this or any other designe."

176–178. "The Prince of *Wales* by comming in Person discouered our plot, and found how faire so euer we pretended, wee meant nothing lesse. . . ."
The Second Part of Vox Populi, p. 22.

180. "*Francis Quicchardino* (a man so sufficient, as the very reckoning of his worth and perfections would require a story) saith of them: The Spanish Nation are covetous and deceitfull, and where they bee at libertie, exceedingly outragious, tyrannous, and very proud and insolent. And *Andrew*—a famous Senatour of *Venice*, saith of them; That they are unfaithfull, ravenous, and the most insatiable of all Nations: For where is it (saith hee) of all the places of the world, where these infamous Harpies set their feet, which is not defiled with the foot-steps of their most abhominable vices."
An Experimentall Discoverie of Spanish Practises
(1623), pp. 30–31.

APPENDIX A

DOCUMENTS RELATING TO "A GAME AT CHESSE"

1.

"A new play called *A Game at Chess*, written by Middleton" was licensed by Sir Henry Herbert, June 12, 1624. So his Office Book MS.[1]

> [MS. note by Malone in his copy of quarto III in the Bodleian Library (Mal. 247).]

2.

GEORGE LOWE *to* SIR ARTHUR INGRAM *at* YORK

1624, Aug. 7. London. . . . There is a new play called the *Game at Chess* ("Chestes") acted yesterday and to-day, which describes Gondomar and all the Spanish proceedings very boldly and broadly, so that it is thought that it will be called in and the parties punished.

> [*Historical MSS. Commission, Report on MSS. in Various Collections*, vol. VII: The MSS. of the Hon. Frederick Lindley Wood, p. 27.]

3.

MR SECRETARY CONWAY *to the* PRIVY COUNCIL

May it please your LL.ps —

His Ma.tie hath receaued informačon from the Spanish Am-bassado.r, of a very scandalous Comedie acted publickly by the King's Players, wherein they take the boldnes, and p̄sumption in a rude, and dishonorable fashion, to represent on the Stage the persons of his Ma.tie, the King of Spaine, the Conde de Gondomar, the Bishop of Spalato &c. His Ma.tie remembers well there was a commaundment and restraint giuen against the rep̄sentinge of anie modern Christian kings in those Stage-plays, and wonders much both at the boldnes

---

[1] Fleay (*Hist. of the Stage*, p. 268) seems to indicate that the "play called *The Spanishe Viceroy*," mentioned in the letter of submission from the King's Men to Herbert on December 20, 1624 (see *Variorum Shakespeare*, vol. III, pp. 209–10), is to be identified with *A Game at Chesse*. But, as it is specifically stated in the letter that that play was acted "not being licensed under your worship's hande," this is impossible. Cf. no. 10 below.

nowe taken by that companie, and alsoe that it hath ben per-
mitted to bee so acted, and that the first notice thereof should
bee brought to him, by a forraine Ambassado^r, while soe
manie Ministers of his owne are thereaboutes, and cannot but
have heard of it. His Ma^{ts} pleasure is that yor LL^{ps} p̄sently
call before yo^u as well the Poett, that made the comedie, as the
Comedians that acted it, And upon examinac̄on of them to
com̄it them, or such of them as yo^u shall find most faultie, unto
prison, if yo^u find cause, or otherwise take securitie for their
forthcominge; And then certifie his Matie what yo^u find that
comedie to bee, by whom it was made, by whom lycenced,
and what course yo^u thinke fittest to bee held for the exem-
plarie, and severe punishment of the p̄sent offendors, and to
restrayne such insolent and lycencious p̄sumption for the
future.

This is the charge I haue receaued from his Matie And wth
it J make bold to offer to yor LL^{ps} the humble service of

Yo^r LL^{ps}

most humble servant

EDW. CONWAY

Rufford
August 12, 1624.

[State Papers (Dom.), James I, vol. 171, no. 39.]

4.

Amerigo Salvetti, Florentine Ambassador, to Picchena,
August 23, 1624 [English Style, August 13]

Da otto giorni in qua, si recita in questa città da questi
comedianti publici, quasi ogni giorno una comedia che loro
chiamano il giuoco degli scacchi; nella quale rappresentano
al vivo tutte le azioni del Conte di Gondemare, durante il
tempo che fu qui Ambasciatore, non lasciando nulla adietro,
che in loro oppinione gli paia di scuoprire, come dicono le
suoi machinazioni et falzità con tanto applauso et concorso
di questo popolo, che si crede, che ogni volta che l'hanno
recitata habbino i comedianti guadagnato da 300 scudi di oro.
Vi introducono ancora l'Arcivescovo di Spalatro, et in som-
ma è una cosa molto satirica, et che dà grandissimo gusto. Si
crede nondimeno che sarà prohibita subito che il Re n'habbia
notizia; perchè non possono tanto lacerare il Conte di Gonde-

mar nel scuoprire la sua maniera di trattare, che non dipinghino contro lor voglia per huomo di valore, et consequentemente, che non refletta fiachezza sopra di quelli che gli davano credenza, et che giornalmento trattavano seco etc. [*B.M. Add. MS.* 27962. *c.* p. 189.]

5.

SIR FRANCIS NETHERSOLE *to* CARLETON, *August* 14, 1624

...Yet we have now these ten dayes a new play here, the plot whereof is a game of Chesse, under wch the whole Spanish businesse is ripped up to the quicke, and Gondomar brought on the stage in his chayre, wch fecheth skorners so well that the players have gotten 100^ll the day knowing ther time cannot be long.

[*State Papers (Dom.), James I*, vol. 171, August 1624, no. 49.]

6.

PRIVY COUNCIL, sitting of August 18, 1624

A warrant directed to Ralph Robinson one of the Messengers of his Ma^ts: Chamber to bring Middleton before theire LLo^pps to Answer &c./

[*P.C. Register, James I*, vol. VI, 424: printed in the Malone Society *Collections*, vol. I, p. 380.]

7.

SIR FRANCIS NETHERSOLE *to* CARLETON, *August* 19, 1624

...The players were yesterday called before some of the LL of ye Counsell who met here for that purpose by whom they are forbidden to play any more at all till they may be licensed agayne by his Ma^ty, and must appeare agayne at his returne from his Progresse, for wch they have put in bonds.

[*State Papers (Dom.), James I*, vol. 171, August 1624, no. 60.]

8.

AMERIGO SALVETTI, FLORENTINE AMBASSADOR, *to the* SECRETARY, August 30, 1624 [English Style, August 20]

La comedia, che rappresentava il Conte di Gondemar è stata dipoi prohibita da questi Signori consiglieri di Stato, per ordine venuto di Corte, dove si crede, che l'Ambasciatore di Spagna si fusse fatto sentire.

[*B.M. Add. MS.* 27962. *c.* p. 191.]

A Game at Chesse

9.

ALVISE VALARESSO, VENETIAN AMBASSADOR, *to the* DOGE AND SENATE, August 30, 1624 [English Style, August 20]

In one of the public mercenary theatres here they have recently given several representations under different names of many of the circumstances about the marriage of the Infanta. The work is of no great merit from what they say, but it drew great crowds from curiosity at the subject. The Spaniards are touched from their tricks being discovered, but the king's reputation is much more deeply affected by representing the case with which he was deceived. The Spanish Ambassador has made a remonstrance, and it is thought that they will at least punish the author.

[*Cal. of S.P. (Ven.)* 1623–1625, no. 577.]

10.

PRIVY COUNCIL, sitting of August 21, 1624

A lr̃e to Mr Sec: Conway.

After &c Accordinge to his Mats pleasure signified to this Board by yor lr̃e of the 12th of Aug: touching the suppressing of a Scandalous Comedie, Acted by the Kings Players, We haue called before vs some of the principall Actors & demanded of them by what lycence and Authoritie, they have p'sumed to Act the same, in answere wherevnto they produced a Booke being an Orriginall and perfect Coppie thereof (as they affirmed) seene and allowed by Sr Henry Herbert kt Mr of the Reuells vnder his owne hand, and subscribed in the last page of the said Booke We demanding further whether there were noe other pts or passages represented on the Stage then those expressly contayned in the Booke, they confidently protested that, they added or varied from the same, nothing at all The Poett they tell vs is one Middleton who shifting out of the way, and not attending the Board wth the rest, as was expected We have giuen warrant to a Messengr for the Apprehending of him. To those that were before vs we gave a sound and sharpe reprooff making them sensible of his Mats high displeasure herein, giving them straight Charg and Com͞and that they presume not to act the said Comedie any more, nor that they suffer any Plaie or Enterlude whatsoever to be acted by them or any of their Company, ontill his Mats pleasure be furder knowne. We have Caused them lykewise to enter into a Bond for their Attendance vpon the Board, whensoever they shalbe called, As for our Certifying unto his Ma: (as was intimated by yor l͞re) what passage in the said Comedie we should fynd to be Offensive and Scandalous, we have thought it our duties for his Ma^{ts} Cleare informac͞on, to send herewth all the Booke it selfe subscribed as aforesaid by the M^r of the Revells, that soe either yor selfe, or some other whom his Matie shall appoint to ⸱puse the same, may see the passages themselues out of the Orriginall, and call Sr Henry Herbert before yo^u to know a reason of his lycensing thereof who (as we are given to vnderstand) is now attending at Court, soe having doone as much as we conceived agreeable wth our duties in Conformitie to his Maties Royal Commandm^{ts}, and that wch we hope shall giue him full satisfacc͞on, We shall contynew our humble prayers to Almightie God for his health and safetie. And bid yo^u very &c./

[*P.C. Register, James I*, vol. VI, 425: printed in the Malone Society *Collections*, vol. I, pp. 380–81. Also in the *State Papers* (*Dom.*), *James I*, vol. 171, no. 64. The text printed by the Malone Society is preferable for its accuracy.]

11.

CHAMBERLAIN *to* CARLETON, *August* 21, 1624

... I doubt not but you have heard of our famous play of Gondomar, wch hath been followed wth extraordinarie concourse, and frequented by all sorts of people old and younge, rich and poore, masters and servants, papists and puritans, wise men etc. churchmen and statesmen as Sr Henry Wotton, Sr Albert Morton, Sr Beniamin Ruddier, Sr Thomas Lake, and a world besides; the Lady Smith would have gon if she could have persuaded me to go wth her, I am not so sowre or severe but that I wold willingly have attended her, but that I could not sit so long, for we must have ben there before one o'clocke at farthest to find any roome. they counterfeited his person to the life, wth all his graces and faces, and had gotten (they say) a cast sute of his apparell for the purpose, wth his Lytter wherin, the world sayes lackt nothing but a couple of asses to carrie yt, and Sr George Peter, or Sr T. Mathew to beare him companie. but the worst is in playeing him, they played somebody els, for wch they are forbidden to play that or any other play till the K^s pleasure be further known; and they may be glad yf they can so scape scot-free: the wonder lasted but nine dayes, for so long they played yt.

> [*State Papers (Dom.*), *James I*, vol. 171, August 1624, no. 66. The text printed in Birch's *Court and Times of James I*, vol. II, pp. 472–473 and copied by Bullen, vol. I, p. lxxxiv contains several serious blunders.]

12.

MR SECRETARY CONWAY *to the* PRIVY COUNCIL

Right honorable

His Matie havinge receaued satisfacōon in y^r LL^ps indeavours and in the significaōon thereof by yo^rs of the 25 of this p̄sent, hath commaunded mee to signifie the same to yo^u. And to add further, that his pleasure is, that yor LL^ps examine by whose direcōon, and applicaōon the personnating of Gondomar, and others was done. And that beinge found out, that partie or parties to bee severely punished. His Matie beinge unwillinge for ones sake, and only fault to punish the innocent or utterly to ruine the Companie. The discovery on what partie his Mat^s Justice is properly, and duly to fall, and yor execuōon of it, and the accompt to be retorned thereof, his Matie leaues to yor LL^ps wisdomes & care. And this beinge that I haue in charg, continuinge the humble offer of my service and dutie to the attendance of yor commaundments J remaine

Yo^r LL^ps

most humble

Servaunt

Woodstock   EDW. CONWAY

 August 27, 1624.

> [*State Papers (Dom.*), *James I*, vol. 171, August 1624, no. 75.]

13.

The EARL *of* PEMBROKE *to the* PRESIDENT *of the* COUNCIL

My very good Lord,

Complaynt being made unto his Ma^ty against ye Company of his Comedians for Acting publiquely a Play knowne by the name of a Game at Chesse Contayning some passages in it reflecting in matter of scorne and ignominy upon ye King of Spaine some of his Ministers and others of good note and quality. His Ma^ty out of ye tender regard hee has of that Kings hono^r, and those his Ministers who were Conceived to bee wounded thereby, Caused his letters to bee addressed to my LL and ye rest of his most hon^{ble} privy counsell, thereby requireing them to Convent those his Comedians before them and to take such Course with them for this offence as might give best satisfac̄con to ye Spanish Ambassado^r and to Their owne Honnors. After examinac̄con, that hon^{ble} Board thought fitt not onely to interdict them ye playing of that play, but of any other also vntill his Ma^{ty}: should give way unto them; And for their obedience herevnto they weare bound in 300^{li} bondes. which punishment they had suffered (as his Ma^{ty} Conceived) a Competent tyme; upon their petic̄on delivered here unto hym, it pleased his Ma^{ty} to comaund mee to lett yor Lo^p: to impart to ye rest of that hon^{ble} Board. That his Ma^{ty}: nowe Conceives ye punishment if not satisfactory for all their Insolency, yet such, as since it stopps ye Current of their poore livelyhood and maintēance without much prejudice they Cannot longer vndergo. In Com̄iserac̄on therefore of those his poore servants, his Ma^{ty}: would have their LL^{ps}: Connive at any Common play lycenced by authority, that they shall act as before; As for this of ye Game at Chesse, that it bee not onely antiquated and sylenced, but ye Players bound as formerly they weare, and in that poynt onely never to Act it agayne; Yet not withstanding that my LL proceed in their disquisic̄on to fynd out ye originall roote of this offence, whether it sprang from ye Poet, Players, or both, and to Certefy his Ma^{ty}: accordingly And so desireing yor Lo^p to take into yor Considerac̄on and them into yor Care; J rest

Court at   Yo^r Lo^{ps} affectionate
  Woodstock the   Cousin to serve you
  27th of August   PEMBROKE
    1624./

[*B.M. Egerton* MS. 2623 f. 28: reduced facsimile in *Shakespeare's England*, vol. 1, facing p. 296.]

14.

ALVISE VALARESSO, VENETIAN AMBASSADOR, *to the* DOGE AND SENATE, Sept. 6, 1624 [English Style, Aug. 27]

The comedians who presented what I reported have been condemned not to perform until further order. The Council pronounced this sentence, the king having referred the case to them. He willingly refers such cases to them in order to give them some employment and rid himself of the odium of such decisions.

[*Cal. of S.P.* (*Ven.*) 1623–1625, no. 568.]

15.

PRIVY COUNCIL, sitting of August 30, 1624

A warrant directed to Robert Goffe one of the Messengers of his Ma^{ts} Chamber to bring one Midleton sonne to Midleton the Poet before theire Llo^{ps}: to answer &c./

[Privy Council Register, James I, vol. VI, 429; printed in the Malone Society Collections, I, p. 381.]

16.

PRIVY COUNCIL, sitting of August 30, 1624

This daie Edw. Middleton of London gent. being formerly sent for by warrant from the Board tendred his Appearance, wch for his Indempnitie is here entred into the Register of Councell Causes nevertheless he is enioyned to attend the Board till he be discharged by Order from their lo^{pps}:/

[Privy Council Register, James I, vol. VI, 429: printed in the Malone Society Collections, vol. I, p. 381.]

17.

After nyne dayse wherein I have heard some of the acters say they tooke fiveteene hundred Pounde the spanish faction being prevalent gott it supprest the chiefe actors and the Poett Mr. Thomas Middleton that writt it committed to prisson where hee lay some Tyme and at last gott oute upon this petition presented to King James

> A harmles game: coyned only for delight
> was playd betwixt the black house and the white
> the white house wan: yet stille the black doth bragge
> they had the power to put mee in the bagge
> use but your royall hand. Twill set mee free
> Tis but removing of a man thats mee.

[Written in an old hand in a quarto of the play in the Dyce Collection at South Kensington (no. 6561, shelf-mark 25, D. 42). Printed in Dyce's edition of Middleton, vol. I, p. xxxv.]

APPENDIX B

Actus Quintus

SCE^A. PRIMA

The Black-Knight (in his Litto^r) & ye Bl: B^{ps} Pawne aboue: Then
ye Black-house, (meeting the white Knight, and white Duke.

Bl. K^t. Is the *Black-Bishop's Pawne,* the *Jesuite*
   planted above for his Concise *Oration*?
Bl. B^s. P. Ecce Triumphanti, Me fixum Cæsaris Arce.
Bl. K^t. Ar't there (my *holy Boy*?) Sirha: *Bishop Tumbrell*
   is Snap'd i'th' *Bag* by this time.   5
Bl. B^s. P. Hæretici pereant sic.
Bl. K^t. All lattin? sure the *Oration* hath infected him.
   Away: make haste; they are Coming.
Bl. B^s. P. Si quid mortalibus vnquam Oculis hilarem, et gratum
   aperuit Diem, Si quid peramantibus Amicorum Animis Gaudium 10
   attulit, peperituè Lætitiam (Eques Candidissime-prælucentissime)
   fælicem profectò Tuum, a Domo Candoris, ad Domum Nigritudinis
   Accessum, promisisse, peperisse, attulisse fatemur. Omnes Aduentus
   Tui conflagrantissimi, Omni qua possumus Lætitia, Gaudio,
   Congratulatione, Acclamatione, Animis obseruantissimis Affectibus 15
   diuotissimis, Obsequijs Venerabundis Te Sospitem Congratulamur.
Bl. K. Sir! In this short *Congratulatorie Speeche*
   You may conceive how the whole *House* affects you.
Bl. K^t. The *Colledges,* and *Sanctimonious Seede-Plotts.*
wh. K^t. 'tis cleere: and so acknowledgd (*Roiall Sir*)   20
Bl. K^t. Harck (to Enlarge your *Welcom*) from all *Parts*
   is heard sweet-sounding *Aires: Abstruse-Things* open,
   of voluntary *freenes*: and yond *Altar*   ⎧ *An Altar*
   (*the Seate of Adoration*) seemes t'adore ⎨ discovered with
   the Vertues you bring with you.   ⎪ *Tapors on it*: and 25
wh. K^t. There's a Taste   ⎩ *Images* about it.
   of the *old vessell* still.
wh. D. th' *Erronious Rellish.*

A Game at Chesse

Song.

Wonder *work some strange-Delight*
30   *(this Place was neuer yet without)*
To welcom the faire *white-House-Knight,*
        and to bring our Hopes about.
*May from y*ᵉ *Altar,* *Flames* *aspire*
Those *Tapers,* *set themselues on fire:*
35   *May senceles Things our* *Joies approue,*   ⎧ *The Images*
        and those *Brazen-Statues* *moue*   ⎨ *moue in a*
        quickend by some Powre aboue;   ⎩ *Dance.*
        or what more strange to show our Loue.

    *Bl. K*ᵗ. A happie *Omen* waytes vpon this howre:
40   All *Moue* (portentously) the *Right-hand* way.
    Bl. K. Come, let's sett free, all the most choice delightes
        that ever adornd daies, or quickend Nightes—

                                    Exeunt/

SCEᴬ. SECUNDA:

*The white Queenes Pawne, & Black-Bishop's Pawne. Then y*ᵉ *Black Queenes-Pawne: Then y*ᵉ *white Bishop's Pawne, & y*ᵉ *Bl. Knights Pawne.*

    *wh. Q*ˢ. *P.* I see 'twas but a Triall of my dutie now,
        'hath a more modest Mind, and in that Vertue
        most worthelie hath *Fate* provided for Me:
        Hah! 'tis the Bad Man in the *Reuerend habit*
5   dares he be seene agen (Traitoʳ to Holynes)
        oh Marble fronted Impudence, and knowes
        how Ill 'hath vsd me! I'am ashamd he blushes not.
    *Bl. B*ˢ. *P.* Are you yet stoard with any womans pittie?
        Are you the *Mistris* of so much devotion,
10   Kindnes, and Charitie, as to bestow
        an Almes of *Loue*, on your poore *Suffrer*, yet?
    *wh. Q*ˢ. *P.* Sir, for the *Reuerend Respect* you ought
        to give to *Sanctitie* (though none to Me)
        in being her *Seruant* vowd, and weare her Livory:
15   Yf I might councell you, you should nere speake
        the Language of Vnchastnes in that *Habit*,
        You would not thinck how ill it doth with you.
        The world's a Stage, on which all *Parts* are plaid,

168

you'lld thinck it most Absurd to see a devill
presented there, not in a devills shape   *20*
or (wanting one) to send him out in yours,
you'lld raile at that for an Absurdetie
no *Colledge* ere Coḿitted: for decorum-sake, then
for Pitties cause for sacred Vertues hono^r,
yf you'll persist still in your devills-Part   *25*
present him, as you should doe: and Let one
that Carries vp the Goodnes of the *Play*
come in that Habit, and I'll speake with him.
Is there so litle hope of you, to smile (Sir)?
Bl. B^s. P. yes: at your feares: at th' Ignorance of your Powre, *30*
the litle vse you make of Time, youth, *Fortune,*
Knowing you haue a *Husband* for *Lusts* shelter,
You dare not yet make bold with a *Frends* comfort.
This is the plague of weakenes.
wh. Q^s. p. so hot burning   *35*
the Sillables of *Sin* fly from his Lipps
as if the Letter came new-cast from Hell.
Bl. B^s. P. Well: setting a-side the dish you loath so much
(which hath byn hartely tasted by your Betters,
I come to *Marrie* you to the Gentleman   *40*
that last enioyd you: I hope that pleases you!
there's no imodest Rellish in that office!
wh. Q^s. P. strange, of all Men, he should first light on him
to Tye that holy *Knot,* that sought t'vndoe me!
were you requested to performe that Busynes (Sir?)   *45*
Bl. B^s. P. I name you a sure Token.
wh. Q^s. P. As for that (Sir)
Now y'ar most wellcom: and my faire hope's of yo^u
you'll never break that sacred *Knot* you tye once.
with any lewd Solliciting hereafter.   *50*
Bl. B^s. P. But all the crafte's in getting of it knit:
you are all one fire to make your Cozoning Market:
I am the *Marrier,* and the *Man;* doe you know me?
doe you know me (nyce-*Iniquitie, Strict Luxurie,*
and *holy whoredome,*) that would clap on *Marriage*   *55*
with all hot speed to soalder vp your *Game?*
See what a Scourge *Fate* hath provided for Thee.
You were a *Maid,* sweare still: y'ar no worsse now
I left you as I found you: haue I startled you?
I am quitt with you now for my discovery,   *60*
Your Out-cries, and your Cuñings: farewell *Broccadge.*

wh. Q^s. P. nay, stay, and heare me but give thancks a litle
    (yf your eare can endure a work so gratious)
    then you may take your pleasure.
65 *Bl. B^s. P.* I haue don that.
wh. Q^s. P. That Powre that hath preseru'd me from this devill
Bl. B^s. P. how?
wh. Q^s. P. This: that may Challenge the Cheif *Chaire* in hell,
    and sit above his *Master*!
70 *Bl. B^s. P.* Bring in *Merit*!
wh. Q^s. P. That sufferdst him, (through Blind lust) to be ledd
    last night, to the *Action* of some *Comon-Bed.*
Bl. Q^s. P. within}. Not over-Comon neither.
Bl. B^s. P. hah! what voice is that.
75 *wh. Q^s. P.* of *Virgins* be thou ever honored:
    You may goe now: you heare I haue given Thancks Sir)
Bl. B^s. P. Heere's a strange *Game*: did not I lye with you?
within}. Noe.
Bl. B^s. P. what a devill art thou?
80 *wh. Q^s. P.* I will not answeare you (Sir)
    after Thanckes-giving.
Bl. B^s. P. why, you made promise to Me
    after the *Contract*! And you were prepar'd for't!
    and set your Joies more high!
85 *within}.* Then you could reach (Sir)
Bl. B^s. P. This is a Bawdy *Pawne*; I'll slytt the throat on't.
Bl. Q^s. P. What! offer violence to your Bedfellow?
    to one that workes so kindly, without *Rape*?
Bl. B^s. P. my Bed-fellow!
90 *Bl. Q^s. P.* doe you plant your Scorne against me?
    why, when I was *Probationer* at *Bruxells*,
    that Engine was not knowne. Then *Adoration*
    filld-vp the Place; and wonder was in fashion:
    Is't turnd to the wild Seed of Contempt so soone?
95   can five yeeres stamp a *Bawd*? It is no longer (Sir)
    since you were cheif Agent for the *Transportation*
    of Ladies daughters, yf you be remembred:
    Some of their *Portions* I could name: who pursd 'em too:
    They were soone disposesd of worldly Cares
100   that came into your fingers.
Bl. B^s. P. shall I heare her?
Bl. Q^s. P. Holy derision, yes: till thine Eare swell:
    whose [child] Neice was she, you poysond with child
      twice,

and gave her out possessd with a fowle Spirit
when 'twas indeed your *Bastard*?   *105*
Bl. B^s. P. I am Taken
in mine owne Toiles.
wh. B^s. P. yes: and 'tis Just you should be.
wh. Q^s. P. And thou (lewd *Pawne*) the shame of Womanhood
Bl. B^s. P. I am lost of all hands.   *110*
Bl. Q^s. P. And I cannot feele
the waight of my *Perdition*, now He's taken,
it hath not the Burthen of a Grashopper.
Bl. B^s. P. Thou whore of *Order, Cockatrix in Voto*,
Bl. K^{ts}. P. yond's the *white-Bishop's Pawne*: I'll *Play* at's Hart
now.   *115*
wh. Q^s. P. how now (*Black-Villaine*) wouldst thou heape a
Murder
on thy first fowle offence? oh *Merciles Blood-hound*
'tis time that thou wert Taken,
Bl. K^{ts}. P. how? prevented?
wh. Q^s. P. for thy sake, and that *Partner* in thy *Shame*   *120*
I'll neuer know Man farther then by *Name*.—*Exeunt.*

Features peculiar to this MS. and to the texts of the class to which it belongs:

1. Massed stage-directions at the head of the scene. The stage-directions in the text, such as those found at v, i, 23–26, 35–37 and v, ii, 73, 78, and 85 do not occur in the Folio texts of *The Two Gentlemen of Verona* and *The Merry Wives of Windsor*.

2. The omission of passages found in the longer versions. These occur between ll. 20 and 21 of v, i, ll. 11 and 12, 28 and 29, in the middle of ll. 83 and 95, and between ll. 102 and 103 of v, ii.

Characteristics of Crane as a transcriber:

1. The expansion of certain contracted forms. Where Middleton writes *thei're*, *Ime*, and *'tis* Crane often has *they are* (v, i, 8), *I'am* or *I am* (v, ii, 7, 110) and *it is* (v, ii, 95). This fact should make one sceptical of certain metrical tests for ascertaining dates and authorship, unless one is sure of the nature of the texts to which they are applied.

2. A preference for certain forms of common words. Where Middleton writes *has* and *youde*, Crane writes *hath* (v, i, 7 and ii, 2, 3, 7, and 113) and *you'lld* (v, ii, 19 and 22). This fact, also,

leads one to regard with suspicion the test for determining authorship by the frequency of a particular form of a common verb or pronoun.

3. Crane is profuse and consistent in his use of italics. Middleton does not employ the distinction between the secretary and italic hands, but uses a mixed hand throughout. In the early part of the Trinity MS. there is what seems to have been an attempt to distinguish words that would have been printed in italics by writing them slightly larger and more upright, but the attempt was soon abandoned, and there is no sign of it in Middleton's part of the Bridgewater-Huntington MS.

4. Crane uses emphasis capitals more frequently and more consistently than does Middleton.

5. Crane's punctuation is much fuller and more careful than Middleton's. One has only to put Crane's version of v, i, 8:

> Away: make haste; they are Cōming.

beside Middleton's:

> Awaye, make haste, theire coming

to realise this. A careful comparison of v, ii, 90–100 with the Trinity MS.'s version of the same speech will make this point still clearer.

Further, one may almost say that the two men use two different systems of punctuation. The use of exclamation and interrogation marks is practically the same in both texts, but there the likeness ends. Commas suffice for Middleton where Crane uses commas, brackets, and colons. Middleton does use brackets, but far less frequently than Crane, and practically only for a vocative, while Crane uses them for most of the purposes set out in pp. 87–97 of Mr P. Simpson's *Shakespearean Punctuation*. Middleton very rarely uses a colon (for two examples see v, i, 50 and v, ii, 83) but Crane is very fond of them. Middleton often places a comma at the end of a speech, but in the main he employs a semi-colon for all the heavier stopping (he even ends a scene with a semi-colon) where most people, including Crane, would use a full stop, which Middleton uses only occasionally.

These facts make it clear that (as the author would probably be the first to acknowledge) Mr Simpson's book on *Shakespearean Punctuation* is a compendium of all the usages of the period, rather than the system employed by Shakespeare or any other single person. Furthermore, that the scribe should pay so much more attention than the author to the punctuation and the capitals makes it doubtful that the system employed should have been intended specially as a guide to a speaker (rather than for a reader), although one readily admits that the punctuation of that age is more rhythmical, and less logical, than that of the present day.

F I N I S

For EU product safety concerns, contact us at Calle de José Abascal, 56–1°, 28003 Madrid, Spain or eugpsr@cambridge.org.

www.ingramcontent.com/pod-product-compliance
Ingram Content Group UK Ltd.
Pitfield, Milton Keynes, MK11 3LW, UK
UKHW020324140625
459647UK00018B/1998